THIS IS
MAURITIUS

THIS IS
MAURITIUS

Alain Proust

Text by Alan Mountain

First published in 1995 by
New Holland (Publishers) Ltd
London • Cape Town • Sydney • Singapore

The author and publishers wish to thank Yves Halbwachs for his
generous assistance.

ISBN 1 85368 556 9

New Holland (Publishers) Ltd
24 Nutford Place,
London W1H 6DQ

Managing editor: Mariëlle Renssen
Editor: Anouska Good
Art Direction: Janice Evans and Petal Palmer
Design and DTP: Darren MacGurk
Map: Loretta Chegwidden
Reproduction by Hirt & Carter (Pty) Ltd, Cape Town
Printed and bound in Singapore by Tien Wah Press (Pte) Ltd

PHOTOGRAPHIC CREDITS

CONTENTS

MAURITIUS PROFILE

PORTRAIT OF MAURITIUS

INDEX 159

Frontispiece: The striking peak of Montagne du Rempart dominates the surrounding landscape.
Title page: The tranquil waters and unspoilt beach at Trou aux Biches is typical of much of the Mauritian coastline.
Left: Undulating hills and wide plains of sugar cane are a feature of the island.

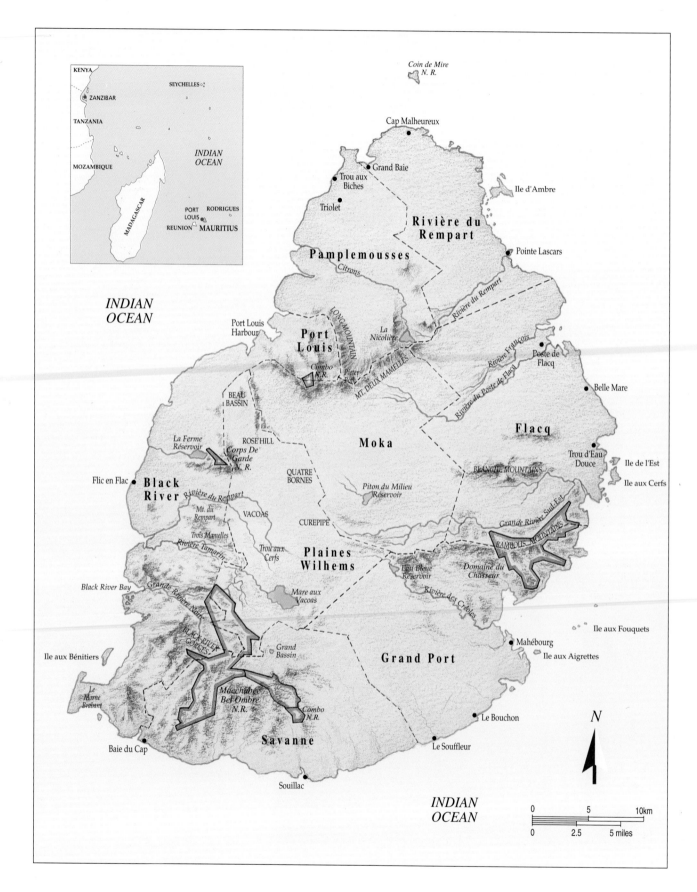

KENYA

SEYCHELLES

ZANZIBAR

TANZANIA

INDIAN
OCEAN

MOZAMBIQUE

MADAGASCAR

PORT   RODRIGUES
LOUIS
REUNION   MAURITIUS

Coin de Mire
N. R.

Cap Malheureux

INDIAN
OCEAN

Grand Baie

Trou aux
Biches   Ile d'Ambre

Triolet   **Rivière du
                                   Rempart**

Port Louis   Pointe Lascars
Harbour
             Pamplemousses
                    Citrons   Rivière du Rempart

                                        Rivière François
             **Port   La
             Louis**   Nicolière   Poste de
                                                           Flacq

LONG MOUNTAIN   Combo   Rivière du Poste de Flacq   Belle Mare
                     N.R.   Pieter
BEAU   Both   MT. DEUX MAMELLES
BASSIN
                                                                Flacq

La Ferme   ROSE HILL   **Moka**   BLANCHE MOUNTAINS   Trou d'Eau
Réservoir   Corps De   Douce
                 Garde   Ile de l'Est
Flic en Flac **Black   N. R.   QUATRE   Piton du Milieu   Ile aux Cerfs
              River**   BORNES   Réservoir
                        Rivière du Rempart   Grande Rivière Sud Est
                     Mt. du   VACOAS
                     Rempart   BAMBOUS MOUNTAINS
                  Trois Mamelles   CUREPIPE   Domaine du
                  Rivière Tamarin   **Plaines**   Eau Bleue   Chasseur
                             Trou aux   **Wilhems**   Réservoir
Black River Bay   Cerfs   Rivière des Créoles
           Grande Rivière Noire
                              Mare aux   Ile aux Fouquets
                              Vacoas
Ile aux Bénitiers   Mahébourg
              BLACK RIVER   Grand   Ile aux Aigrettes
              GORGES   Bassin   **Grand Port**
Le
Morne   Le Bouchon
Brabant   Macchabée
               Bel Ombre   Combo
               N.R.   N.R.   Le Souffleur
                        Savanne
Baie du Cap

                    Souillac   **INDIAN
                                                               OCEAN**

                                                    N

                                        0   5   10km

                                        0   2.5   5 miles

MAURITIUS PROFILE

The first view the air traveller has of Mauritius is of an emerald-green island set in the deep blue of the vast Indian Ocean. Situated just north of the Tropic of Capricorn, 20° 15' south of the Equator and 57° 35' east, this small pear-shaped island was once an active volcano that formed part of a chain stretching from Réunion in the south to the Seychelles in the north. Over time the original volcano has been severely eroded so that Mauritius today bears little resemblance to the cone shape typically associated with most volcanos.

Arab traders first came upon the island in the 10th century, but they did not stay and so the island remained forgotten behind a curtain of ignorance until the beginning of the 1500s when it was discovered by the Portuguese during their epic voyages of discovery. They, in turn, used the island as a victualling stop on their way to Goa and Malacca but did not settle. At the end of that century, the Dutch landed and named the island after Prince Maurice of Nassau. They stayed, intermittently, for a little over a century before they too decided to leave. It was the French, arriving in 1715, who stayed and gave the island its essentially French character and charm. However, as a result of the conflict between the British and French in Europe and the rivalry in their respective trade with India, the British attacked the French garrison stationed on the island and defeated the defenders. From that time until independence in 1968 the island was administered by the English.

The island's present inhabitants are descendents of settlers from Europe, slaves from Africa and Madagascar, and indentured labourers and artisans from Asia, with each racial group bringing its own culture and traditions. These different attributes have, over time, become uniquely blended to create a national harmony which recognizes diversity within a common identity and national character. Today, the island has a population of 1,1 million people which makes Mauritius the most densely populated country per unit area in the world.

Since independence, Mauritius has emerged as a successful model of socio-economic development. After an initial period when the island was gripped in a stranglehold of poverty, high unemployment, a mono-crop (sugar) economy and unsustainable population growth, the economy has been diversified and today manufacturing has become the island's most important industry, followed by sugar production and tourism. Family planning and population development rank high on the country's national agenda and in 1990 it was awarded the Population Award by the United Nations Population Fund. As a result of these achievements the island has full employment and its general standard of living is steadily improving.

Nevertheless, it is the natural beauty of the island, its warm all-year-round climate, white beaches, tranquil sea, exciting deep-sea fishing, excellent hotels and friendly people that make Mauritius such an attractive tourist destination.

LAND AND SEA

When time stood still

Many millions of years ago the earth's crust burst open and some of its molten innards gushed out and piled up on the floor of what is now the Indian Ocean. As the boiling lava steadily cooled, a chain of roughly hewn, conical-shaped land masses formed, creating a string of volcanic peaks which protruded from the surface of the sea. Slowly Nature sculpted those stark peaks in many different ways and in the process bequeathed a sprinkling of beautiful islands.

One of those islands is Mauritius. While it is true that the pristine beauty of that jewel has become tarnished since the arrival of man upon its shores nearly five hundred years ago, its deep lustre and innate sparkle nevertheless remains intact. The island is roughly pear-shaped and occupies an area of approximately 1 865 square kilometres. At its longest point Mauritius is only some 62 kilometres and at its widest a mere 48 kilometres. Skirting the island is a perimeter of coastal lowlands which never rise beyond 350 metres above sea level and vary in width from a little under 2,5 kilometres in the south to 15 kilometres in the north. The centre of the island is characterized by a central plateau that ranges in height from 350 metres to 700 metres above sea level. The plateau, which is almost imperceptible as you cross the island, slopes relatively steeply in the south and in places terminates in black basalt cliffs. These stand guard against the strong winds and rough seas sometimes conjured up by the southeasterlies. In the north, the central plateau melts away into broad coastal lowlands.

Geologists believe that the central plateau is all that remains of the floor of the volcano that gave birth to Mauritius. Conspicuous evidence of the island's volcanic origin is to be found in a number of features. Firstly, there are small extinct volcanic craters, such as the one at Trou aux Cerfs near Curepipe in the centre of the island, and at Kanaka in the south. Secondly, there are a few volcanic lakes, such as Grand Bassin, which is situated near the Savanne mountains in the south and is considered a sacred lake by the Hindus of Mauritius. And, lastly, countless round volcanic rocks have been collected by farm labourers over centuries and piled into huge mounds or neatly stacked into large mausoleum-shaped squares in order to begin clearing the land for agriculture.

The mountains

In a few places the walls of that ancient volcano have been able to resist the onslaught of Nature's weathering, and the monuments to this are the island's mountains with their pointed and striated peaks. In the north there is the Moka range which can be traced for some 20 kilometres, starting at Mount Ory and finishing at Nouvelle Découverte. It is within a basin created by these mountains that Port Louis, the capital of Mauritius, is situated. The Moka range is well known for its three peaks – Guiby Peak, Le Pouce (the thumb) and Pieter Both, the tallest at 818 metres; it was named after Admiral Pieter Both who drowned in 1615 when his ship and three others belonging to the Dutch East India Company were caught in a tropical cyclone. They ran for the safety of Port Louis, but just a few kilometres short of their destination they were swept towards the rocks at Baie du Tombeau. Three of the four ships were wrecked with great loss of life. Pieter Both's ship, the *Banda*, was swept south and eventually smashed to pieces on the barrier reef at present-day Albion, north of Flic en Flac. Crowning the summit of Pieter Both Mountain is a peculiar, rocky protrusion which resembles a human head that seems to be precariously attached to the cloak-shrouded shoulders of a man. Legend has it that should this head become dislodged from its body, some great disaster will befall Mauritius and the island will be destroyed in its entirety. Fortunately, however, geologists tell us that the likelihood of this happening is remote – indeed it is more likely to wear down than fall down!

Along the west coast and stretching down to the south is the Black River chain. Here the domineering La Montagne du Rempart (785 metres) and its companion peaks, the Trois Mamelles, (Three Breasts) create a serried range which, from a distance, look like the dorsal fin of a giant sleeping dragon. Further south on the way to Le Morne lies Piton de la Rivière Noire which, at 840 metres, is the highest mountain in Mauritius. Guarding Le Morne peninsula is Le Morne Brabant, which provides an impressive backdrop to one of the

Mauritius is an elite tourist destination that offers its visitors powder white beaches, translucent, coral-encrusted lagoons and sophisticated resort hotels. Inland rises a central plateau, dominated by the jagged peaks of Montagne du Rempart and Trois Mamelles.

island's finest beaches. Continuing from there to the southeast, past Piton du Fouge, is the Savanne mountain range, with Piton Savanne (705 metres) providing the highest point. Lying in the southwest on the undulating slopes which gradually reach up to the Savanne mountains is an area of approximately 1,5 hectares on which nothing grows. Here the intriguing coloured earths of Chamarel are to be found; these earths are made up of seven separate but contiguous bands, with each one having a different colour. It is believed that their different hues are the result of their volcanic origin and the uneven cooling of the molten rock.

In the northeast are the Bambous mountains which extend from the centre of the island to the east coast, providing a fine backdrop to Grand Port bay, on the shores of which the town, and once important naval port, of Mahébourg is situated. There are two important peaks in this range – Mount Bambous and Mount Lion; the latter is the most striking, as it looks just like a lion resting, waiting, watching...

To the north of the Bambous range are the mountains of Blanche and Fayence, which are hardly mountains, but rather collections of occasional hills that often only just manage to raise their diminutive but delightful heads above the surrounding sugar cane.

While the mountains of Mauritius do have some places where the wit and skill of serious mountain climbers may be challenged, they are better known for the hiking trails they offer those who want a change from the beach. There are a number of hikes, lasting from a few hours to a full day, which traverse some of the uncluttered parts of the island and offer hikers a brisk challenge and a contact with nature that's laced with lovely views. Through breaks in forest patches, or as the hiker crests a summit, beautiful vistas open up across broken valleys, over rolling sugar fields and on to the distant turquoise sea beyond. Many of the best walks are in the mountains in the south, but for those who may have an urge to gain a bird's-eye view of Port Louis, a walk up Le Pouce, the thumb-shaped peak which stands prominently

Le Morne Brabant is an impressive peak that stands in eternal watch over the Le Morne peninsula in the southwest corner of the island. At times, when rain clouds are low, it is sullen and brooding, but often the sun's early rays reflect its varied colours.

behind the city, should suffice. Here magnificent views of the city, of adjacent Pieter Both Mountain and the interior of the island can be had.

Coral reefs – the island's barrier against the sea

An almost continuous barrier of coral reef virtually encircles most of the island, the only extensive gap being in the south of the island between Souillac and just to the north of Le Souffleur where some of the island's major rivers flow into the sea. Coral reefs can only survive in salt water which has a reasonably high level of salinity (20ppt); therefore, where there is a preponderance of rivers bringing fresh water into the sea – as happens in this area – coral reefs tend not to occur. Furthermore, there is only a narrow continental shelf and the drop-off is steep, thus there is little to dampen the sea's ardour, and wave action in this region is known to be intense.

Coral reefs are made up of hard corals of the Order *Scleractinia*. These comprise massive structures built by tiny anemone-like organisms (polyps) which produce external calcareous skeletons. Some large corals, such as the mushroom coral, are solitary but most form colonies whose skeletons lock together to form a wide variety of shapes – some

weird, some graceful, some busy and some intricate, but all fascinating. The creation of corals paradoxically comes about in death. When corals die many of the polyps' skeletons remain intact and are fused together, thereby adding to the reef. Small cracks and holes within the basic structure steadily fill with sand and the calcareous remains of other reef plants and animals. Gradually a solid limestone structure is formed, while all the time new polyps keep growing on its surface. Thus only the outermost layer of the growing reef is alive. These reef-building corals, or what scientists call *hermatypic corals*, require a great deal of sunlight, warm water temperatures (over 20°C, for most of the year), full marine salinity, water that has little sediment in it, and a stable, hard sea floor onto which they can attach themselves. Microscopic plants called *zooxanthellae* are of great importance to the growth and health of corals. Millions of these minute organisms are packed into the living tissues of most reef-building corals. Although reef corals capture plankton from the water, a significant amount of their food comes directly from the *zooxanthellae*. It is for this reason that the most prolific coral growths are in the shallow, well-lit, nutrient-rich waters that the *zooxanthellae* prefer.

Coral reefs have been traditionally classified into four types, depending on their stage of development. They are fringing reefs, barrier reefs, patch reefs including banks and shoals, and atolls. Fringing reefs normally start as narrow platforms which extend outwards from the shore. Over time, as the platform expands further into the sea, it grows in size and depth, usually to between 15 and 45 metres, depending on factors such as the profile and depth of the seabed and the clarity of the water.

Barrier reefs occur along the edges of islands or continental shelves and are substantial structures. The major difference, apart from size, between barrier and fringing reefs is that barrier reefs are separated from the shore by a wide lagoon. Barrier reefs normally evolve from fringing reefs. As the seaward margin of the fringing reef grows and keeps pace with the surface of the sea, it extends out from the land until it reaches an optimum depth, whereupon it turns to run more or less parallel with the shore, thereby creating an off-shore lagoon. With the passage of time the narrow coral platform that connects the reef to the land becomes exposed and, as the level of the sea rises and falls according to the movements of the earth, it ceases to grow and eventually dies. The reef's umbilical cord is thus

severed and nature soon removes the debris, leaving behind a living and independent barrier reef that is able to protect the island from all but the worst of the sea's bad tempers.

Coral reefs can develop at any place where the underlying rock has at some time been close enough to the surface of the sea for coral growth to occur. Then, as sea levels rise or geological changes cause the seabed to drop, coral patches, banks or shoals are left behind.

Atolls, Charles Darwin once postulated and modern geological research vindicates, represent the final or mature stage of coral-reef building around volcanic islands. Here, the island may sink below the surface of the sea due to geological forces. Or, according to Nature's immutable plan, the erosive forces of sun, wind and rain relentlessly bombard the island, gradually wearing it away until it eventually disappears below the surface of the sea in total submission. What is left behind is a circular outer coral reef and a shallow inner lagoon: in other words, an atoll.

Within the coral lagoons that surround Mauritius there is a kaleidoscope of colour and a world of infinite fascination. The visitor to this silent world will be amazed by the incredible shapes and forms the different corals take. Among these, staghorn coral (*Acropora spp.*) is

spiky with many branches that resemble the antlers of a stag bull; it grows quickly and is an early colonizer of disturbed areas. Sometimes the staghorn coral is confused by the uninitiated with the knob-horned coral (*Pocillopora verrucosa*), which also has many branches but these are flattened and have knob-like projections. A very common coral in Mauritius is the plate coral (*Leptoseris sp.*) comprising flat, plate-like sheets, some up to a metre in diameter, which spread out in layers across the reef. The mushroom coral (*Fungia scutaria*) looks like the underside of an upturned mushroom and consists of a single, huge polyp which is either oval or elongate. The juvenile coral is attached to the reef by a short stalk, but adults break loose and lie on the bottom of the sea and often divers think they are dead and remove them. There are many varieties of honeycomb coral in Mauritian waters. These are round and boulder-like and are completely covered with moderately large corallites (the skeleton of the polyp) which, instead of projecting out as in most corals, are sunken into the surface. The walls of touching corallites fuse together in such a way that they form a honeycomb pattern. Some of the species to be looked for in this genus in Mauritius are: *Favites spp.* (honeycomb coral), *Favia spp.* (false honeycomb coral), *Anomastrea irregularis* (irregular honeycomb coral), and *Acanthastrea echinata* (spiny honeycomb coral). The labyrinthine brain coral (*Platygyra daedalea*) and the various related brain corals are other common residents in the coral reefs of Mauritius. These corals occur subtidally (the sea area below that affected by tide movement) and form large, flat, slab-like or hemispherical colonies, the surface of which is convoluted like a brain. Other common corals are the turbinate coral (*Turbinaria mesenterina*) which consists of a trunk that expands into a large table-like crown that spirals at its centre (hence the name turbinate which is derived from *turbo*, the Latin for a whirlpool or spinning top). The turret coral (*Dendrophyllia aurea*) is interesting in that it is more akin to an anemone in appearance and behaviour than to a coral. It consists

The coral reefs that virtually encircle Mauritius and its outlying islands have a rich marine life, which includes not only a wide variety of colourful tropical fish, but also spectacular gorgonians, soft corals and a multitude of other fascinating organisms.

of a number of cylindrical branches which end in large corallites within which there is a single, large, golden polyp. This has tentacles that radiate out, making it particularly easy to confuse the coral with an anemone. These are only some of the corals that make up the fascinating barrier reefs of Mauritius; there are many others.

Divers who have had a chance to assimilate some of the beauty and fascination of this silent world should pause for a moment and watch the vividly coloured and patterned reef fishes at their daily task of feeding. Reef fishes can be divided into three categories, depending on the type of food they eat. There are the herbivores – those which feed on marine plants; the omnivores which feed on plants and animals; and those that feed on animals only – the carnivores. Most species of coral reef fishes are carnivores and each has its special way of hunting its prey. Eels, for example, slither stealthily through narrow crevices and cracks in the reef or through sand and rubble lying on the floor of the sea, using their sense of smell to seek out their prey. Once found, eels seize their quarry with their long needle-like teeth and quickly consume it. They are not voracious eaters and are happy to spend time hidden in their holes with only their heads showing, seemingly watching the passing scene. The well-camouflaged scorpionfishes, the deadly stonefishes, lizardfishes and flatheads find a strategic position where they blend into their background and patiently wait for their prey to come unwittingly by. With amazing swiftness the hapless victim is seized and consumed and the deadly vigil resumes as if nothing had ever happened. Groupers and snappers swim about the reef, apparently disinterestedly, hoping to lull their prey into a false sense of security, but then lunge with deadly speed when the opportunity arises. The goatfishes, with their drooping barbels (so reminiscent of a traditional Chinese mandarin with his long drooping moustache), busily vacuum the reef's floor using their barbels to constantly probe and dislodge buried crustaceans and small fishes. These are then sucked up, inevitably

Coral reefs are some of Nature's most imaginative creations. Whilst separate coral families can be identified in terms of their structure, their shape and form is never exactly the same. Many fascinating hours can be spent snorkelling along the reefs that line the island's shore.

with other debris, which is rapidly sorted and then puffed out in a small cloud of residue from the fish's mouth. Emperor fish slowly glide across the surface of the reef looking for any sign of movement that may betray the presence of buried prey. Once detected they pounce on the unsuspecting victim, quickly consume it and then move on to continue scanning the reef. Rays rest on the floor of the lagoon or in a cove in the reef where the

Goldies decorate the reefs while the deep blue sea provides a radiant backdrop.

floor is flat and sandy. Here, with the help of the sea, they excavate into the sand seeking buried molluscs which they crush with their teeth. Some types of fish are parasitic, such as the cleaner wrasses, which are specialized feeders that live off the parasites and damaged tissue of other larger fishes. Then there are fish who cheat. They copy the cleaner wrasses and, using the opportunity this gives them to get in close, quickly bite off a tasty morsel from their unsuspecting victim and flee before it has time to retaliate.

Although Mauritius's underwater world has much to amuse, to intrigue, to fascinate and to impress its visitors, it is tragic that its value was not understood by the people and the authorities earlier. In the quest for food, shells, corals and marine specimens to sell to tourists and to export, much damage has been done. In some instances nature rapists have even resorted to the use of dynamite and large sections of the coral reefs have been destroyed. It is pitiful and frustrating to dive in God's coral kingdom and see it laid waste by thoughtless and greedy Man. In much of Mauritius it is only in the remote corners, where man's corrosive tentacles have not yet spread, that the true nature of the island's reefs can be fully experienced.

However, concerned underwater sport enthusiasts and conservationists have formed the Mauritius Underwater Group and the associated Mauritius Marine Conservation Society which have campaigned strenuously for these practices to be stopped. Investigations are also underway for the establishment of a number of marine parks and the first to be established may possibly be at Blue Bay, near Plaisance in the south of the island. Much has been done, but much still needs to be done before the wounds of the past are fully healed. Controls have been introduced by the authorities to restrict the removal of shells and other items from the sea, but more should be done to enforce these controls. Conservationists also urge tourists not to buy shells from vendors who may approach them clandestinely on the beach. With these measures, combined with Nature's extraordinary ability to forgive and to restore, a slow healing process has begun.

Natural forests – depletion of a rich heritage

Before man first set foot on the soils of Mauritius, the island was covered in thick luxuriant forests which clad the central plateau and the slopes of the mountains with tall hardwood trees. In the valleys and along the rivers there were dense thickets of bamboo, the beautiful fan-shaped traveller's palm, or ravenale (*Ravenala madagascariensis*), which was introduced from Madagascar during the 19th century, various tree ferns and a variety of forest shrubs and shading canopy trees. There were also natte trees (*Labourdonnaisia glauca*) and the famous tambalacoque or dodo tree (*Sideroxylon grandiflorum*). The large half-smooth, half-rough seeds of this tall tree with a silver trunk are so hard that it is almost impossible to crack them. There was a long-standing belief, which science has in recent years accepted as being substantially correct, that before the seed could create life it had to first pass through the digestive system of the dodo bird (*Raphus cucullatus*), as its gizzard abraded and softened the shell of the seed, so enabling it to break out and germinate. However, with

the advent of man, all this changed. The dodo became extinct and the tall hardwood trees, of which the tambalacoque and the Mauritian ebony (*Diospyros tessellaria*) were major species, were cut down in great numbers because they made excellent timbers for the repair and manufacture of boats on the island and for export as raw logs. Furthermore, with the demise of the dodo, the germination of the seeds of the tambalacoque tree was no longer possible and thus in the last 300 years, no new trees of this species have taken root on the island. In a survey of the island done in 1973 only 13 old and dying specimens were found, each estimated to be over 300 years old. (It is interesting to note that there are many instances of plant-animal mutualism known to science in which the elimination of a plant species has affected an associated animal population, but this appears to be the only known example of the reverse.) The depletion of the forests was further hastened by the drive for more and more land on which to plant sugar cane. Today less than one per cent of the original forests remains; most of these are found to the south of Plaine Champagne in the Bel

Ombre-Macchabée forest. As in so many other parts of the world, the ecological value of natural forests was realized too late to save the best areas, but nevertheless strenuous efforts are being made to educate the public on the ecological value of forests and to preserve those few areas that remain. Patches of indigenous forests, some hardly more than a few square kilometres in extent, have been declared nature reserves and have thus been fenced off by the Department of Forestry in order to encourage regeneration and further growth.

Forest reserves in Mauritius are divided into three categories of control and ownership. Firstly, there are Crown Forest Lands, comprising the declared nature reserves as well as certain areas given over to tea planting. Then there is the state-owned 'Pas Géométrique', which is made up of a narrow coastal strip including the island's public beaches. Many lovely sites situated within this area have been leased to the hotel industry. Lastly, there are privately owned remnant forests which are mainly to be found on the upper slopes of the mountains. A 4 000-hectare national park is planned for the beautiful Gorges

The talipot palm (Corypha umbraculifera) in full bloom. This palm, which gets its name from the flowers it bears above the tree like an umbrella, is monocarpic so it will die when flowering is complete. This is usually when the tree is between 40 and 60 years old.

de la Rivière Noire (Black River Gorges) where the last vestiges of prime habitat for Mauritian fauna and flora are located. At present the area is a declared natural area and various conservation measures have been implemented. Since less than one per cent of the island's original forests are still intact today, the need for protection of this area is self-evident.

Although the Mauritian plant kingdom has some 900 species of which nearly one-third is endemic to the island, exotics found their way to the island from the very earliest days of Mauritius's human history. They have brought a riot of colour which lasts throughout the year and helps to soften much of the harshness of human habitation. Notable species include the busy bougainvillea; the alamanda with its bright yellow flowers; the heavily scented, waxy textured frangipani trees which line the streets; as well as hibiscus, strelitzia, anthuriums, orchids, oleanders and poinsettias which grow with gay abandon in the gardens of many homes and in the parks of the towns. Then there are flowering trees and shrubs such as the *Trochetia condolleana* with

One of the afforestation schemes introduced to provide the island with timber and to serve as a conservation measure.

their huge carmine flowers, the *Trochetia triflora*, a shrub with snow-white blossoms, and the *dombeya*, which is a compact shrub with masses of pink flowers.

Lining the beaches are groves of whispering casuarinas (*Casuarina equisetifolia*), or *filaos* as they are known in Mauritius, a name given to them by the Portuguese. Their filigree-like delicacy has been a feature of the Mauritian landscape since the French explorer and cartographer Abbé Alexis Rochon introduced the tree from Australia in 1778. A hundred years later the British governor, Sir Arthur Gordon, recognizing the casuarina's ability to prosper in a salt-laden environment, ordered the planting of the trees around the island as a conservation measure and also to serve as windbreaks.

Other exotic trees include a variety of acacias, coconut palms, the albizia, the Indian almond (or *badmanier*) and the fascinating Indian banyan (*Ficus benghalensis*), which has a proliferation of aerial roots that reach down to the ground and then reroot themselves.

Birdlife

In earlier times, when the island was covered in verdant mountain forests and the streams ran free of man's pollution, an estimated 26 species of birds once lived here. Of these the dodo is the best known – for the perverse reason that it was a large conspicuous bird and one of the first to become extinct soon after man came into contact with it (giving rise to the archetype expression for extinction, 'as dead as a dodo'). The bird and this tragic reflection on man's careless nature have been immortalized in Lewis Carroll's famous book *Alice's Adventures in Wonderland*. The name 'dodo' is derived from *doudo*, the Portuguese word for 'silly', which no doubt reflected the early mariners' contempt for the unfortunate bird. These feelings still persist amongst many people even to this day, as they believe that the bird was too stupid to recognize danger and, as the humorist Will Cuppy once wrote, it 'seems to have been invented for the sole purpose of becoming extinct, and that was all he was good for'. The large round bird, about the size of a goose,

*A recreation of the famous dodo bird (*Raphus cucullatus*) on display in the Natural History Museum in Port Louis.*

was a member of the pigeon family. It lived on the fruits of the ebony tree, and because it had no natural enemies it no longer had use for its wings, which steadily became smaller in relation to the size of its body. Eventually the disproportion became so great that the dodo could no longer fly. Thus when the first sailors arrived on the island, the bird had no means of escaping from them. And having had no enemies, the birds did not fear these new arrivals, so their capture and destruction was easy. The seafarers, suffering from scurvy and a lack of fresh meat, caught them and ate them. However, it is said that they did this without relish because the birds were reputed to be tough and tasteless. This was not enough, however, to fight off more insidious enemies – pigs and dogs (introduced to the island by the early Dutch settlers) which preyed on their eggs, and rats which the Portuguese had inadvertently brought in nearly a century before. The death knell for the dodo came when its essential food, the seed of the ebony tree, virtually disappeared as the last of the host trees were cut down and turned into the spars and cargo of passing ships. By 1693, less than one hundred years after the Dutch had colonized Mauritius, the dodo was no more. All that remains are the sketches of the bird made by passing mariners, and one foot and a bird's head. The foot is in the London Natural History Museum and the head is in the Oxford University Zoology Museum. A replica of the bird, refurbished recently by the Royal Museum of Scotland in Edinburgh, can be seen in the Mauritius Natural History Museum in Port Louis.

Mauritius still possesses some incredibly rare and important bird species, but they could be as doomed as the dodo if the present conservation efforts to protect them are not successful. The Mauritius Kestrel population, for example, has suffered from the deterioration of habitat resulting from pesticide poisoning and from hunting. Before the Mauritius Kestrel Conservation Program was introduced in 1973, the population had declined to a mere four birds. Today the number exceeds 200 birds in the wild, with an estimated 35 breeding pairs. The world's rarest parakeet, the Echo Parakeet, is endemic to Mauritius and it too is under considerable threat. In 1992 there were estimated to be around 15 birds in the wild. Since 1985 the Mauritius Wildlife Appeal Fund has been funding and managing a project to breed these birds in captivity in order to boost their numbers. Other endemic birds, all of which sadly are threatened in some way or another, are the Pink Pigeon, the Mauritius Cuckoo-Shrike, the Mauritius Black Bulbul, the Mascarene Paradise Flycatcher, the Mauritius Fody and the Mauritius Olive White-eye.

Fauna of the island

The only mammals indigenous to Mauritius were two species of fruit bat, one of which is now extinct, and three species of insectivorous bats. The surviving fruit bat, known as the Mauritius Golden Bat or flying fox because of its looks and size, is relatively common. It is to be found at nightfall swooping over highland forests in search of fruit. It is considered to be a delicacy by the locals as its flesh, sweetened by its sugar-cane diet, is used to make a curry speciality. The Dutch colonists introduced the Tundjuc deer from Java as a means of supplying meat to the settlers and to

Situated in the north of the island, Grand Baie is largely protected from the prevailing southeast winds and so offers holiday-makers near-perfect conditions throughout the year.

passing ships. Today deer farming is well established in the Case Noyale and Le Morne areas. Deer hunting takes place annually, mainly on the estates of the Franco-Mauritians. However, at beautiful Domaine du Chasseur, an estate on the southeast coast, the owners have introduced controlled fee-paying hunting as an income and management measure.

The Dutch also introduced pigs which, over time, lost their domesticity and have reverted back to nature. Wild-boar hunting has become a favourite pastime among some Mauritians. The Portuguese introduced the Macaque monkey in 1528 from Malaysia and these are to be found in relatively large troops in the Black River area. From Madagascar came the tenrec, an insectivorous creature that looks like a hedgehog, but has no tail. Mongooses were brought in from India in 1900 in order to help control the rat population of Mauritius, but they multiplied at such a rate that they too have become a nuisance.

Before the arrival of settlers on the island, Mauritius had a large giant tortoise population. But these ponderous reptiles, like the dodo, had no defence against the intruders who came in ships and who killed them off for their meat and the oil in their livers. Eventually the giant tortoise faced total extinction on

all the Indian Ocean islands, but fortunately by the end of the 19th century they had become a protected species – thanks, *inter alia*, to the research and lobbying of Charles Darwin.

The giant tortoise was reintroduced to Mauritius when specimens were imported from Aldabra, a group of islands belonging to the Seychelles, where the tortoises had been left largely undisturbed on some of the islands making up the group. Zebu cattle, noted for their humpback, were imported from Madagascar and today they can still be seen pulling large-wheeled carts along the streets of the island to the delight of an ever-increasing number of tourists.

Climate

Mauritius lies just north of the Tropic of Capricorn, some 20 degrees south of the equator. While the island is technically within the tropics and is often subject to high temperatures and humidity levels during summer, it has a maritime subtropical climate. A number of ameliorating factors helps to reduce the impact of these high temperature and humidity levels: cooling winds that blow off the sea and the altitude of the inland plateau help to reduce temperatures, on average, by some 5°C. It is for this reason, combined with the prevalence of malaria

Deer hunting takes place on a number of privately owned estates, particularly in the south of the island.

along the coast, that those who could afford it preferred to live inland on the plateau at places like Curepipe rather than at the coast. With the advent of modern air conditioning and the eradication of malaria, this situation has changed, however. There is little consistency in Mauritian weather – it can be raining in Curepipe but bone dry on the coast. Likewise weather on the east coast is different to that of the west coast. The former is usually much windier and wetter, particularly in January and February when the prevailing winds

drive in from the southeast, the latter drier and hotter. As is to be expected in the southern hemisphere, the hottest months are those of January to April, when temperatures range between 25°C to 35°C. During these months tropical cyclones periodically unleash their ferocious might on the island. While cyclones of varying magnitude occur annually it is usually only once every 15 years or so that a really big one passes over the island. Looking back over the last 50 years this has been more or less the pattern. A severe storm occured in 1945. In 1960 Cyclone Carol ravaged the island, and in 1975 this happened again when Cyclone Gervaise passed over Mauritius in its savage meanderings across the Indian Ocean. At the time of writing (November 1994) a prolonged drought and unseasonal high temperatures could be the portents for another onslaught.

The cooler months are July to September when day temperatures average 24°C and night temperatures 16°C. Mauritius does not have a specific rainy season but it generally rains less during the cooler 'winter' months, June through to September. For the holidaymaker, especially those who come from cooler climes and who long for the warmth of the sun, it is hard to imagine a more amenable climate!

The Mauritian climate, with its relatively high year-round temperature and regular rainfall, is well-suited to the growing of sugar, and cane fields dominate the Mauritian landscape.

PATTERNS OF THE PAST

Early beginnings

During the 10th century, Arab sailors who used to ply the seas between India and the east coast of Africa came upon an island which they called *Dina Harobi* – meaning literally 'Abandoned Island'. The reason for giving the island this name will never be known for sure, but Mauritian historians believe that it was probably because the island had been hit by a cyclone prior to their arrival and was lying prostrate, devastated by the wind's unseen might. Indeed, they postulate that the same cyclone could have been the reason for the Arab sailors being so far off their normal course. These early seafarers did not try to take the island for themselves; instead they passed on and left only their rough maps and their experiences as legends for historians to ponder. It is argued that the words *Dina Harobi* were corrupted over time to *Dinarobin*, the word normally associated with the Arab name for Mauritius. The corrupted word is believed to mean 'Silver Island'; it is said by some that the Arab sailors sighted the island at midday, silver in the distance as it danced on a shimmering sea.

For the next 500 or so years the island remained lost in obscurity, locked behind the shutters of ignorance. However, with the advent of the great voyages of discovery which began in the Middle Ages it was the Portuguese, having pioneered a route around the Cape, who were the first Europeans to visit the island. According to the latest study on the subject (by Mauritian historian, Alfred North Coombes) it was Diego Dias, the brother of the famous Bartolomeu Dias de Novaes and a companion of Vasco da Gama (when he managed to reach India on 20 May 1498), who rediscovered the island. He was the captain of one of a fleet of ships commanded by Pedro Alvares Cabral, which was on its way to India around 1500. The fleet had become dispersed after passing through a severe storm while rounding the southern tip of the African continent. Four ships of the fleet were lost in the storm and Dias's ship was blown far south and then east by the

The ill-fated St Géran *ran aground on Ile d'Ambre in 1744. This monument at Poudre d'Or stands in memory of all those who lost their lives that tragic night.*

Westerlies. After getting out of the grip of the wind, and on his way back westward towards the African coast where he hoped to meet up with the remainder of the fleet, Dias came upon three islands which historians believe to be Rodrigues, Mauritius and Réunion. He was able to confirm their positions on the rough maps that da Gama had been given by an Arab pilot he had met at Malindi on the east African coast and who had guided him to Calicut on his epic voyage to India. Thus on the map of Cantino, which is dated 1502, the three islands of Rodrigues, Mauritius and Réunion are fairly accurately positioned.

The intrepid explorer and navigator Diego Fernandez Pereira was the next to visit the island, in 1507, while looking for a less dangerous route to India, east of Madagascar. (The islands and unchartered atolls in the Mozambique channel were a danger to the Portuguese ships.) He named the island *Isla do Cerne* (Swan Island), either after his ship, believed to be of the same name or, some say, because of the dodo which he may have likened to a swan. In or about 1528, Don Diego Rodrigues landed on Rodrigues, the island which still bears his

name to this day. Together with Réunion and Mauritius he named the island group the Mascarenes, after the Portuguese admiral Don Pedro Mascarenhas.

The Portuguese made no attempt at permanent settlement on any of the three islands as they already had a base on the island of Mozambique, off the east coast of the African mainland. Their sailors, however, used the island as a place of refuge during stormy weather as they laboriously ploughed their way on the long voyages to and from India. They also brought cattle, pigs and monkeys to the island so that when their ships called there, they could obtain fresh meat supplies. It is believed that it was during the Portuguese period of occupation – from 1507 to 1539 – that rats first reached Mauritius. Thought to have escaped from the ships, and having no natural enemies on the island and an ability to reproduce their numbers very rapidly, it did not take many years before they became a serious menace.

The Dutch arrive – the island's first settlers

After the Portuguese abandoned the idea of establishing a sea route to India east of Madagascar, a decision taken in or about 1539, they had no further use for Mauritius and so the island remained unoccupied for the next 60 odd years. In 1598 a Dutch fleet of five ships on its way to Batavia, under the command of Vice Admiral Wybrandt Van Warwyck of the Dutch East India Company, was blown off course by heavy winds and accidentally came upon Mauritius. The Dutch sought shelter in the large bay they saw in the southeast corner of the island and landed at a place known today as Vieux Grand Port, near present day Mahébourg. Warwyck named the bay after himself, and the island Mauritius, after Prince Maurice of Orange and Nassau, the Stadtholder of Holland. The Dutch considered the island to be ideally situated as a refreshment station along their trade routes to India and to Java (or Batavia) in the east. Timber and fresh water were plentiful and the rich volcanic soils were good for agriculture. However, they did not attempt to colonize the island to any great extent.

Instead they only bothered to develop small temporary settlements along the southeast coast. However, in order to pre-empt any attack from the French or English, they did also establish a small military presence at Noordt Wester Haven (North West Harbour), which is where the present Mauritian capital, Port Louis, is situated today.

In 1638 the Dutch East India Company took over control of Mauritius and the first settlers arrived. Their main job was to harvest the hardwood ebony trees they found on the island because timber prices were high in Europe. The Dutch also introduced sugar cane from Java, which they planted in cleared forest areas and from which they produced a potent arrack. They imported slaves from Madagascar and brought in convicts from Java to work on the fields. However, many settlers left for the Cape of Good Hope in 1652 when Jan van Riebeeck established a base there for the Dutch East India Company. The island's isolation, its inadequate harbour and the ravages of the rats left behind by the Portuguese, among other things, led the Dutch to abandon their settlement in 1658. However, in 1663 the Dutch East India Company, regretting its decision to depart from Mauritius,

The Coat of Arms, featuring the now-extinct dodo and a stag (indicative of the deer introduced by the Dutch), is strongly evocative of the island's past.

decided to retake possession of the island in order to prevent it from falling into enemy hands, and on 24 August 1663 they instructed the Governor of the Company's settlement in the Cape to send an expedition to Mauritius. On 20 May 1664, the *Waterhoen* left with 12 men under the command of Jacobus van Nieuwland to reestablish a base on the island. Dutch occupation of the island continued uninterrupted until 17 February 1710 when their last governor, Abraham Momber van de Velde, left the island on the *Beverwaart* bound for Batavia. He left behind depleted forests, neglected sugar-cane fields and angry runaway slaves who were forced to live a beachcomber existence.

The French follow and stay

In 1715, Captain Dufresne d'Arsel took possession of the island in the name of the King of France and renamed it Ile de France. In 1722 the first colonists landed at Warwyck Bay, which was renamed Port Bourbon. However, because of the frequency of strong winds and the difficulties ships experienced in getting through the narrow gaps in the coral reefs, the French abandoned Port Bourbon and moved their maritime operations to Noordt Wester Haven, which they renamed Port Louis. In 1735 the French East India Company appointed Bertrand François Mahé de Labourdonnais, a man of great energy and foresight, to governorship of the island. He immediately set about digging French roots deeper into the soils of their new possession. The new governor formally laid out Port Louis and transformed it from a primitive harbour to a thriving sea port. Sugar cane was cultivated on a large scale in order to produce sugar for export to France. Labourdonnais planned to import the first sugar mill which, transported by the ill-fated *Saint Géran*, went down with the ship which was wrecked on Ile d'Ambre in 1744. However, he later obtained new equipment which was installed on his own estate, La Villebague. Indigo, rice and cotton were planted and a vigorous road-building programme was initiated. Extermination drives against the island's prolific rat population were introduced

Pierre Poivre was the first governor appointed by the French government after the island was taken over from the Compagnie des Indes Orientales in 1767.

and these continued right into the next century (the records for 1826 reveal, for instance, that '830 000 of these destructive animals were caught and destroyed' in that year alone!). More slaves were imported from Madagascar and Africa in order to provide labour on the new sugar estates and other farming lands. Warwyck Bay was successively renamed Port Sud-Est, Port Bourbon and Port Impérial. In 1804 Governor Decaen started a new town at a place known before as Pointe de la Colonie, which he named Mahébourg in honour of Mahé de Labourdonnais, whose bronze statue now stands prominently at Place d'Armes (now renamed Place Sookdeo Bissoondoyal) in Port Louis, overlooking the harbour.

By 1746 Port Louis had become well established as a maritime base and the Compagnie des Indes Orientales (French East India Company) were able to do good business supplying French ships with stores and supplies for their campaigns against the English in India. During the Seven Years War (1756–1763) the Indian Ocean became an extended battleground between the English and the French as their ships battled against one another in the run to and from India. During this war the successors of Labourdonnais, none of whom

had his gift of leadership and control, battled to revictual and supply the French expeditionary forces despatched to India under the orders of Comte d'Arche and Comte de Lally. They received little co-operation from the same men who, 10 years earlier under the command of Labourdonnais, had taken Madras from the English. As a result the French lost the war in India and the government then decided to take over control of the island from the Compagnie des Indes Orientales, whose administration had lasted 46 years (1721–1767), and put it under the charge of the Ministre de la Marine et des Colonies. In addition they appointed a new governor, Pierre Poivre, a man whose vision and drive was equal to that of Labourdonnais, and thus, a new and interesting chapter in the history of the island began.

Pierre Poivre was not only credited for being a good administrator, he was also a keen botanist. He transformed the old Compagnie des Indes nursery at Pamplemousses into a formal botanical garden that was considered to be one of the finest botanical gardens in the world; it still enjoys international recognition today. He sent botanical expeditions to the Moluccas and other places in the East to obtain young plants and seeds of important spices such as cloves, nutmeg and others, which were added to the cinnamon and pepper he had already introduced. His objective was to grow spices on the island in order to help the French break the stranglehold the Dutch had on the spice trade in Europe.

During this time the population of Ile de France began to swell rapidly. From the 800 souls who inhabited the island in 1735, the number grew to 33 539 some 40 years later. According to the official census figures for the year 1776, there were 6 386 people of European descent, 1 999 people of mixed descent and 25 154 slaves who were brought in mainly from Madagascar and, to a lesser extent, from the African continent. The population continued to grow rapidly after this as the sugar industry continued to expand and more and more slaves were brought in.

When the French Revolution took place in 1789, Ile de France was little affected but the local elite, fearing the ideals of the Revolution and the possible effect this could have on their way of life, declared the island independent and broke off relations with France. This unilateral declaration of independence was done at a price since Ile de France on its own had little economic and military might with which it could defend itself. It thus had little alternative but to resort to the 'legalizing' of privateering and to increase trade with neutral countries, such as America and Denmark. During the years 1793 to 1802, no less than 120 privateering expeditions against predominantly English shipping were conducted by the 'bourgeois de marine' of Ile de France. However Napoleon, recognizing the strategic importance of the island in any future war with England, sent General Charles Decaen to the island in 1803 to re-establish French rule there. In honour of his Emperor, Decaen renamed Port Louis, Port Napoléon, while Mahébourg became Port Impérial. As the dark clouds of war began to gather over Europe, little Ile de France was tossed onto the stage of international politics. As long as the island belonged to the French it could offer a secure base in the Indian Ocean from which warships could freely attack

The French fortified Mauritius against attack from the sea. This cannon formed part of a battery positioned at Pointe Aux Canonniers in the northwest to defend the approaches to Port Louis and Grand Baie. No shot was ever fired from it in anger.

laden English ships plying the trade routes between England and India and the East. The island's port could also offer asylum to privateers and corsairs who, sailing under letters of marque, could freely rove the Indian Ocean in search of lonely ships and easy prey. The best known of all the corsairs who operated out of Mauritius was Robert Surcouf, born in 1773 at St Malo in France where he eventually retired, living handsomely from his ill-gotten gains until his death in 1827. Today many of his descendents are prominent and honourable Mauritian citizens.

In order to put a stop to the corsairs, the British government resolved to add Ile de France to their growing empire. In August 1810 a British squadron of four ships sailed into Grand Port Bay to engage a French flotilla of similar size, and a great battle took place within the confines of the navigable water in the bay. An inability to manoeuvre within the restrictions imposed by nature meant that the battle became a gruesome slugging match between the contending sides. There was little room for naval strategy and this made death and destruction the only arbiters in the conflict. Nearly all the ships were sunk or badly damaged, while 141 sailors were

killed and 281 were wounded. Although by other standards this battle may have been considered to be small and remote, it was the only naval battle the English lost during the Napoleonic era. To celebrate their victory, the French had it etched indelibly into the annals of history by inscribing it on the Arc de Triomphe in Paris.

The English resolve to capture Ile de France did not weaken. The island had become too great a risk to their shipping and Napoleon too big a threat to their survival. In December of the same year they came back, but this time better prepared and in much greater numbers. A land force consisting of 12 000 men, composed partly of Indian troops and partly of British soldiers under the command of their general, the Honourable John Abercrombie, set sail from India with a naval task force of 20 vessels of war and a sizable fleet of transport and support ships, under the joint command of Admiral Bertie. Spies warned the French of English intentions and Port Louis, the only port that could offer anchorage to an armada of this magnitude, was converted into a formidable fortress. In addition Pointe aux Canonniers, between Grand Baie and Trou aux Biches in the northwest corner of the island, was fortified and more cannons brought in and pointed seaward to defend the island. But the English, anticipating this move by the French, turned their ships to the island's northeast corner and headed for Cap Malheureux, where they had detected a 400-metre gap in the coral reef. With Port Louis a mere 24 kilometres away it made an ideal place of invasion. While the English armada rode at anchor outside the reef, the army was able to effect a successful landing using small boats to ferry the soldiers ashore. After four days, following brief encounters at Grand Baie, Baie de l'Arsenal and Baie du Tombeau, French resistance ceased and it fell to General Abercrombie to accept the surrender of the French governor, General Charles Decaen. English losses amounted to 150 men dead or wounded, French losses were less.

A new colony of the English crown

At the Treaty of Paris in 1814, Ile de France, Rodrigues and Seychelles were confirmed as British dependencies and once again the island's name changed – this time back to Mauritius. Franco-Mauritians were allowed to retain their language, religion and sugar estates, the Napoleonic legal system was endorsed and Robert Farquhar, the first British governor, recognized the French civil administration system.

The British did not see Mauritius as a place they wished to influence or as a place for settlement and, as a result, the island has remained substantially French in character and charm. The British presence ensured that the island was no longer a threat to their trading routes. The British legacy thus has never extended much beyond the immediate corridors of power.

Throughout the 158-year period that the British administered the island, there was an amicable truce between the French settlers on the one hand, and the English administrators on the other. The French got on with running their sugar estates: their buildings, private homes, cuisine and the games they played were all typical of colonial France, which a century and a half of British control could not change.

In 1835 slavery was abolished, but as the Mauritian sugar industry continued to expand during the 19th century so the need for labourers grew. As a result, the importation of indentured labour from India began in earnest. The island's population started to rise rapidly, with the indentured labourers becoming permanent settlers and their families joining them. By 1865 immigrants from India and their descendents constituted the largest racial group in Mauritius. However, while population numbers rapidly swelled, so a veil of conspicuous poverty steadily descended over the island as the rate of increase in jobs failed to keep up with the number of people seeking employment. The French colonists were largely unaffected by this and they continued to live in grand style. If anything, their lives became easier with the greater abundance of cheap labour. It was not uncommon, for example, for a single household to employ 10 or more domestic servants!

Sugar production dominated the Mauritian economy, to the virtual exclusion of all other forms of economic activity. The island was the largest sugar producer in the British Empire and was affectionately described by Joseph Conrad, who visited Mauritius as a ship's captain, as the 'sugared pearl of the Indian Ocean'. While the island's sugar-based economy expanded, the infrastructure needed to serve the sugar industry improved. A railway network was built and by 1904 more than 200 kilometres of British standard-gauge railway track was laid in order to service the cane producers. (After World War II the rail service was discontinued and the lines were uprooted.) Postal services were improved and post offices built throughout the island, social services were introduced and the harbour at Port Louis was modernized.

Independence comes to Mauritius

In 1936 the Travaillistes, the Mauritian Labour Party, was formed to fight for the rights of the labourers on the sugar plantations. A series of strikes in 1937 and again in 1943 brought the sugar industry to a standstill and the situation was only relieved when the British Government agreed to institute a programme of constitutional reform. In 1948 the first step towards a broadening of the political structure was introduced when the franchise was extended to those who were over 21 years of age and could write their name. During the fifties, the Hindu-dominated Labour Party was

In August 1810 a terrible duel took place between a squadron of four British ships and a flotilla of four French ships on the calm blue waters of Grand Port Bay. This memorial stands in mute remembrance of the lives that were lost in battle.

Within the main courtyard of Government House is a statue of Sir William Stevenson, governor between 1857 and 1863.

led by a medical doctor, Dr (later, Sir) Seewoosagur Ramgoolam, who campaigned tirelessly for the rights of workers. In 1959 the franchise was granted to all adults and a Hindu majority was assured at the polls. The move to political independence from Britain gained a great fillip, but the island moved into a period of political insecurity while sporadic violence broke out on the streets of Port Louis as supporters of the majority Labour Party, who were predominantly Hindu and wanted independence, clashed with supporters of the minority Parti Mauricien Social Democrate (PMSD), who were predominantly Creole (and Franco-Mauritian) and were opposed to independence. While British troops were called in to quell the riots, colonial administrators began to pack their bags and close their files in preparation for their departure.

Nothing could turn the clock back, the colonial era had passed. On 12 March 1968 the Union Jack was lowered for the last time and after more than one and a half centuries, policies for the island were no longer decided in distant England. The country had gained its independence with Seewoosagur Ramgoolam the first prime minister and a coalition government in power.

THE PEOPLE

Mauritius has no indigenous people, only people whose forebears came from elsewhere in more or less recent times. The island's human history began when man had already acquired the ability to build ships and the skill to navigate them across wide and distant seas. People who came to live on the island came from different continents and cultures and Mauritius is thus a human potpourri. It is a fascinating blend of East and West, of black and white, of rich and poor. But from diverse cultures, religions and traditions has come an amazingly harmonious amalgam whose constituent parts, whilst certainly discernible, are by no means divisible.

Here Catholic churches, Hindu temples, Muslim mosques and Buddhist pagodas do not compete but happily form part of the same landscape. Likewise there is an enviable congruence between the people who come from the modest homes of the majority, the colonial mansions of the few and the blend that emerges from the two. Each is a part of the whole and each accepts the other. This cultural and social tolerance brings warmth, colour and an appealing ability to laugh at life. These qualities are infectious and certainly contribute to making a visit to Mauritius a rich and rewarding experience.

In 1990 Mauritius had an estimated population of 1,09 million, which is made up of four different ethnic groups. There are Indo-Mauritians, whose forebears came from India; Creoles, people of mixed ancestry who came from Europe and Africa; Franco-Mauritians, the white descendents of the original French colonists; and Sino-Mauritians, whose forefathers came from China.

Within each of these groups there are further divisions based on culture, religion and language. In order to be able to communicate across this wide spectrum, a lingua franca, Creole, which is a pidgin French and a simple language uncomplicated by difficult grammar and subtle inflection, soon developed. However English, following Britain's long occupation and administration of the island, is the official language of Mauritius.

Indo-Mauritians

Indo-Mauritians are, in the main, descendents of indentured labourers who were brought in from India to work on the sugar-cane fields after the abolition of slavery. Some are the descendents of merchants who followed later and set up businesses independently of the sugar estates. Indo-Mauritians come from three different religious and language groups: Hindi, Tamil, and Muslim. The Hindis come from northern, the Tamils from southern, India. Together they form the largest ethnic group in Mauritius – a little over 50 per cent of the island's total population. The Muslims, who come mainly from the western Gujerati region and Bombay, total an estimated 175 000 persons.

The solidarity and culture of the Indo-Mauritian community is reinforced through religion. Hindu worship is largely a private affair. It may either take place at a secluded spot in a garden where a small shrine is built, sometimes lit by a red light at night, or in a special place in the home. In some Hindu homes it is common to see red flags on bamboo poles displayed outside the house. These are erected to celebrate the birthday and honour of Hanuman, the monkey god who sits in a posture of worship outside Krishna temples.

There are important times, however, when the whole community comes together to celebrate major religious festivals. The Hindu temples and temple-compounds become vibrant and alive with colour as flowers are placed wherever possible and garlands are hung from the statues of different deities. Marquees are erected, flags raised, bamboo shelters appear and open-air cooking areas are set up. Some of the temples' idols are removed from their dark shrines and placed on flower-bedecked chariots and wheeled through the neighbourhood. Others are lifted high onto platforms or onto the shoulders of worshippers and carried ceremoniously around the outside of the temple. Hundreds of deities make up the Hindu pantheon, and as each of them has an auspicious day, a diligent temple committee can have something to celebrate on virtually every day of the year.

Of the major Tamil fesitivals celebrated in Mauritius, the *Cavadee* festival is probably the best known. Observed by the Tamil-speaking Shivite community during the months of January or February when the major *Thaipoosam Cavadee* takes place at most temples throughout the island, this festival honours either the Lord Subramanya (the second son of the god Shiva) or the mother Draupadi. The day of the *Thaipoosam Cavadee* is a public holiday. As part of the celebration, devotees carry a semicircular wooden frame (or *cavadee*) on their shoulders from which pots of milk (*sambos*) and rice are suspended. These are offerings for the deities. The *cavadee* is decorated with bright flowers and peacock feathers. Other devotees carry *goron gon*, large brass pots containing water sanctified by the priest and covered with a large pyramid of flowers. The celebrations normally start at a source of water, be it a river, pond or tap, and then move in a steady procession to the temple where devotees place their burdens in front of the idol. The procession has to maintain a reasonable pace since custom dictates that the milk in the *sambos* should not have curdled by the time they reach the temple. During this time there is a spirit of total submission; participants will

Hindu weddings are always joyous, colourful occasions with brides dressed in elaborate gowns made from brocades, satins and silks. Gold jewellery features strongly, while garlands of flowers and elaborate decorations add to the splendour of the wedding ceremony.

During the Hindu festival of Cavadee *devotees sometimes pierce their tongues and cheeks with needles known as* vels.

have fasted for a couple of days beforehand and their dedication is total. Emotions are heightened by loud, evocative and somewhat piercing music. The devotees become visibly possessed – god-possessed in the eyes of the other worshippers – and are able to perform superhuman feats, such as walking on nail sandals, walking barefoot across long firepits filled with burning coals, pulling carts hitched to meathooks inserted into their backs, or pushing long needles (*vels*) through their cheeks and tongues. Thousands come to celebrate and watch the devotees; the curious are not turned away but may have to jostle with the devout.

The *Maha Shivaratree* is a very important Hindu celebration that takes place over three days at the end of February or mid-March. During this time devout Hindus dressed in white make the pilgrimage on foot to the holy volcanic lake of Grand Bassin in the Savanne mountains to honour the god Shiva. They carry a *kanvar*, a light, arch-shaped wooden or bamboo frame decorated with paper flowers. At the lake pilgrims perform *poojah*, which consists of making food sacrifices either in the water or at shrines on its banks. Others bathe and many take sacred water home. The celebration follows much the same routine as those which take place on the

banks of the Ganges River in India. On the return journey from the lake it is traditional for pilgrims to be given fruit and drinks by the local villagers. One of the days of the *Maha Shivaratree* is an official public holiday.

A Hindu fire-walking ceremony, the *Teemeedee*, takes place throughout the year (although it mostly occurs over the December and January months) and is performed in honour of a variety of gods at various temples throughout Mauritius. The ceremonies are performed after participants have spent an appropriate period of fasting and bathing.

To celebrate the victory of Rama over the evil deity Ravana, Hindus celebrate *Divali*, the Festival of Light. This takes place on an auspicious new-moon night between October and November. The celebration marks the triumph of good over evil and the superiority of knowledge over ignorance. It is a happy and gay occasion during which lamps, traditionally earthenware, are lit throughout the island to symbolize the supremacy of light over darkness. Children let off firecrackers and the family celebrates the event with a special meal and the eating of sweetmeats. The day of *Divali* is an official public holiday in Mauritius.

Ganga Asnan, an optional public holiday on the island, is a purification ceremony that takes place annually. Hindus in great numbers converge on the beaches and enter the sea to purify themselves in its waters and offer gifts to the goddess Ganga. As the Ganges River flows into the Indian Ocean, the sea around Mauritius is considered to carry its sanctity and purifying powers.

At *Ramadan*, during the ninth month of the lunar year, the Muslim faithful do not eat between sunrise and sunset. *Eid-Ul-Fitr*, which marks the end of this period of fasting, is an event of great spiritual significance. After attendance at the mosque, families and friends gather together to celebrate the breaking of the fast. *Eid-Ul-Fitr* is a public holiday.

Creoles

In Mauritius the word Creole is used officially to describe anyone who was born on the island, excluding Indo-Mauritians and Sino-Mauritians. It is effectively, however, used to describe the descendents of African and Malagasy slaves who were brought to the islands in great numbers during the 17th and 18th centuries. The Creole population totals some 340 000 people; they are well known for their sega dancing and music. Sega music originated in the dark days of slavery when a low mournful chant was sung by the slaves to lament their loss of freedom and removal from their homes and loved ones. Over time the inherent rhythm of Africa still coursing through the veins of the people welled up and found expression in movement, and the sega became a traditional dance performed by pairs of the opposite sex. Dances were held on the beach around campfires at night and, because of the thick beach sand, intricate dance steps were tiring and difficult to perform. As a result sega dancing involves an animated shuffling back and forth with the dancers' feet seldom leaving the ground, while their bodies sway seductively in time with the music.

The traditional musical instruments that accompanied the sega were the *ravanne*, a tambourine-like instrument made from goat's skin, the *tantam* which is a guitar-like instrument consisting of a bow to which a gourd is attached and plucked in time to the drum beat, the *maravanne* which comprises a gourd or

Sega dancing is an important cultural feature of Mauritian life.

The colourful 'Dance of the Lion' forms part of Chinese festivites.

box half-filled with stones or dried beans and resembles a maraca, and a steel triangle. Today sega dancing has become a modern and commercialized form of cabaret with beautiful women gyrating their hips in time to music played on electric guitars and keyboards. While the lyrics are in Creole, the traditional laments have given way to witty and sometimes suggestive song. Although the original significance of the sega should never be diminished or forgotten, it has given birth to something uniquely Mauritian that has brought, and still continues to bring, joy to many people.

Franco-Mauritians

Franco-Mauritians make up about two per cent of the total population. Most are direct descendents of the first settlers on the island and their roots go deep into Mauritian soil: it was their forebears who developed the sugar estates and started the island's big businesses, and so wealth and economic power have been historically entrenched in the community. In earlier times most Franco-Mauritians lived in Curepipe on the central plateau, where it was cooler and relatively free from malaria. Most of them had beach cottages which they used at weekends and during winter when it was cooler. However, with the improvement in communications and air

conditioning, the elimination of malaria and the development of shopping facilities and job opportunities throughout the island, there is now no longer such a strong incentive to live on the central plateau, and today Franco-Mauritians live all over the island.

Sino-Mauritians

Sino-Mauritians number around 25 000. In 1826, as a means of obtaining more skilled workers on the island, the British Government invited groups of Chinese artisans to settle there. A number of sailors, artisans and traders took up the offer and settled in Mauritius. Their descendents make up the bulk of the island's Sino-Mauritian community. They have retained the essence of their culture, although many have become practising Catholics. They have also maintained a distinctly Chinese identity within the Chinese quarter of Port Louis, but despite this, they form an integral part of the Mauritian community.

Sino-Mauritians hold key management positions within business and the professions; they also own a variety of businesses, from the local village corner store to large companies. The Chinese Spring Festival, which is held eight days before the Chinese New Year – around the end of January or beginning of February – is still observed. The festival is preceded by a thorough spring cleaning which takes place on the eve of the event; homes are joyfully decorated with lanterns and red streamers (the colour of happiness) inscribed with wishes of peace and prosperity. Firecrackers are let off in order to ward off evil spirits and there is a general atmosphere of merriment. On the following day sweet cakes made from rice and honey are given to family and friends. To honour the occasion the day is an official public holiday.

Catholics

For all of the Catholics on the island, an important shrine is the Church and Shrine of Père Laval at Sainte Croix situated to the northeast of Port Louis. Père Laval was a missionary who arrived in Mauritius in 1841; he was renowned for his campaign for better working and living conditions for the poor on the island. He died in 1864 and was buried in the graveyard of the original church of Sainte Croix where his grave has become a place of pilgrimage. As the French pay homage to the town of Lourdes in southwest France, so Catholics from all over the world come to Mauritius to touch the effigy of Père Laval that is placed on the vault containing his remains outside the new church (built and consecrated in 1968), and to pray for the healing of the sick. A pilgrimage takes place every year during the nights of 7 and 8 September, while on the 9th, the anniversary of the priest's death, Père Laval Feast Day is celebrated when hundreds of people attend mass at the Church of Sainte Croix.

Mauritian architecture

The island's French and British colonial history, combined with its hot and humid climate, manifests itself in interesting and distinctly Mauritian architecture which can be seen in homes ranging from modest bungalows to elegant mansions. Influenced by a blending of French and English colonial architecture, roofs of the elegant homes that were built on the sugar estates tend to be steeply pitched with turrets and dormer windows. Most of the houses are encircled by cool verandahs bordered by fanciful balustrades and intricate cast-iron decoration. Invariably painted white, they create a bold yet tasteful contrast with the vivid greens of the surrounding vegetation and rolling sugar-cane fields. Verandahs play an important social role in Mauritius; they are cool and capture the ambience of outdoor living, providing a place where the family can meet to relax and entertain their guests.

Today, with the steadily rising cost of living, many of the mansions built in bygone eras are beginning to decay, and the signs of deterioration are obvious. Without the abundant and cheap labour of the past, these homes have become an anachronism. Some have been renovated and converted into conference centres, others have become museums, and yet others have been left to contend with the elements – sadly these once grand homes are fighting a losing battle.

Colonial architecture was not limited to the wealthy, however. The poorer sector also incorporated many of its distinguishing characteristics – the high sloping roofs for their insulation against heat, and as a protective measure against cyclones, and the ubiquitous verandah. Today, the nonavailability of hardwood timber and the cost of high-quality craftmanship needed for the verandah detail makes this a very expensive and difficult element to maintain in modern Mauritian architecture. Thus, increasing use of concrete is being made and, combined with the preponderant use of flat roofs as a more effective measure to combat the devastating effects of cyclones, this has resulted in greater functionalism and utility, and regrettably a loss of sparkle in many modern-day Mauritian buildings.

Mauritian cuisine

Traditional Mauritian cuisine evolved over a period of two and a half centuries and is the coming together of the culinary skills of three continents.

It began with the arrival of the early French settlers who brought their European recipes to the island. Over time, these were modified using the tropical fruits and vegetables found locally and oriental spices; and as new arrivals from Africa and Asia brought their recipes, ingredients and cookery skills to their new environment, different ideas were swapped and adapted.

The cornerstone of Mauritian, or Creole, cuisine as it is more commonly referred to, is the curry and the *rougail*. Mauritian curries are many and varied, while *rougail* comprises a tomato-based sauce in which scallions, salted meats, and fish are simmered. This is then served on a mound of rice which is often accompanied by an assortment of chutneys and other condiments.

There are about 25 000 Sino-Mauritians in Mauritius, many of whom are engaged in commerce and have their businesses in colourful Chinatown in central Port Louis.

Mauritius has a number of fine restaurants which would rank extremely well in any international competition. Although seafood is a speciality in many of them, visitors should not ignore Creole dishes on offer. The spicy and unique flavours of the food are to be savoured and will long be remembered as a very pleasurable element of a visit to the island. Other important contributors to Mauritian cuisine are those restaurants which, while recognizing local tastes, are true to the traditions of their home country. It is thus possible to enjoy some of the specialities of France, India and China within a Mauritian ambience.

For those who want a quick bite to eat there are fast-food outlets, some franchised to international fast-food chains and others delightfully Mauritian in notion and content. *Samoosas*, *rotis*, meatballs, soups, noodles, curries, curried rolls and a variety of tropical fruits, often cut into different shapes, can be bought very inexpensively from street vendors.

A tasty delicacy that must not be missed is smoked marlin. This Mauritian speciality has a texture similar to that of smoked salmon, but the colour is a little more beige than pink. It is, however, a delight of equal standing. Available in all supermarkets, smoked marlin is served thinly sliced with each sliver sandwiched between foil so that it can be easily peeled off. For those who prefer tuna it, too, is smoked and is also served in thin slices.

Mauritius has an abundance of tempting culinary delights to offer its visitors.

MODERN MAURITIUS

Post-independence politics

After independence in 1968 the new administration did not have an easy task. The country was poor and entirely dependent on a single crop which was subject to the vagaries of the weather and the uncertainties of a capricious world market. Unemployment was rife and population growth rampant as well as being heavily skewed towards youth – 55 per cent of the population was under 20 years of age; 25 per cent between 25 and 40 years of age; and barely 5 per cent elderly. The burden on the new state's social services was so great that it had virtually collapsed. Furthermore, bedevilling the whole situation was a concomitantly high level of expectation with the new government in power. There was also a strong sense of dissatisfaction and a dangerous perception amongst the disillusioned youth that the government was to blame for all of the country's ills. Not surprisingly political dissension escalated and became increasingly radical with the emergence of the extreme left-wing Mouvement Militant Mauricien (MMM) under the leadership of a young Franco-Mauritian Marxist, Paul Berenger. He had spent his student days in Paris during the heady days of French student politics in the sixties. Berenger returned to Mauritius a socialist crusader to organize the trade unions and to fight for the nationalization of industry, particularly the sugar industry, and the redistribution of wealth to the Indian and Creole peasantry. Predictably the young, particularly the unemployed, flocked to his banner.

To add to the country's woes the price of sugar slumped in the mid-seventies while the price of fuel rose dramatically. The country was caught in the jaws of an economic vice that was tightening remorselessly. In 1979 the government introduced a structural adjustment programme, which was supported by the World Bank and the International Monetary Fund, aimed at diversifying and stimulating the economy while simultaneously introducing specific programmes to tackle the three problems of unemployment, overpopulation and poverty. However, before the reform measures could become fully effective the Ramgoolam administration, accused of corruption and incompetence, was swept from power in a landslide victory by a coalition of Berenger's MMM party and the Parti Socialiste Mauricien led by Mr (later Sir) Anerood Jugnauth in the elections of 1982. However, differences between Jugnauth and Berenger, compounded by an unfavourable reception of their radical policies in important international circles, led to the collapse of the coalition government and to new elections in August 1983.

A five-party coalition formed the new government with Jugnauth as prime minister, and Berenger departed into the political wilderness. In 1986 three Mauritian politicians were found at Amsterdam airport with packages of heroin in their suitcases which led to the opening of a political can of worms in Mauritius. The deputy prime minister resigned from office and the state floundered. Berenger came back into contention and his MMM party forced a new round of national elections on 30 August 1987. Jugnauth won, gaining 39 of the 62 seats in parliament, and the political turmoil of the mid-eighties began to subside. In the general elections held in 1991, a new alliance between Berenger, still leading the MMM party, and Jugnauth heading the MSM (Mouvement Socialiste Mauricien) 0gained a landslide victory at the polls. In 1992 Mauritius became a republic within the Commonwealth and Sir Anerood Jugnauth became the country's first president. The republic also includes Rodrigues, which is politically integrated with Mauritius and several island dependencies, of which Agalega and St Brandon in the Cargados Carajos archipelago are the most important.

Government

Mauritius is a presidential democracy in which the president is the head of state and commander-in-chief. However, full executive power rests with the prime minister who is the head of government. Parliament is the legislative authority in Mauritius. It has 60 members who are elected every five years by popular vote.

Port Louis is the capital of Mauritius. It is a small, bustling harbour city that is growing daily as the economy of the island expands.

All of the major political parties are represented in parliament, reflecting the prevailing democracy of Mauritius. The independence of the judiciary is guaranteed in the Constitution. The legal system is hybrid, being based on both English and French law. Procedural law

A statue of Queen Victoria reflects the colonial influences of the past.

in both criminal and civil litigation is mainly English, whilst the substantive law is mainly based on the French Napoleonic Code. Company law is basically modelled on English law. Many Mauritian lawyers are members of the United Kingdom Inns of Court or graduates of European universities. Mauritius is a member of the International Court of Justice, the International Centre for the Settlement of Investment Disputes (ICSID) and the Multilateral Investment Guarantee Agency (MIGA). It is also a member of most international organizations, including the Commonwealth, the United Nations and most of its agencies, the International Monetary Fund, the World Bank, the African Development Bank, the Organisation of African Unity, and the Indian Ocean Commission.

Education

The island's people have been identified by the Mauritian Government as being their greatest national asset. In terms of the country's National Development Plan, education has to play an increasingly important role in achieving the planned economic growth for the country. To give effect to this the government

has consistently allocated the greatest share of the national budget (13,4 per cent in the 1992/3 fiscal year) to the education portfolio. Today the country enjoys a literacy rate of over 90 per cent and education is free at all 277 primary and 122 secondary schools. Although schooling is not compulsory, the attendance rate is around 90 per cent at the primary level, dropping to an annual average of around 45 per cent at the secondary school level.

Despite the country's educational system being relatively well developed, it is flawed in some respects. The absence of a well-co-ordinated programme of technical and commercial education is one of the main weaknesses of the system. To overcome this, increased funding has been allocated to improving the teaching of science and technical subjects and to improve standards generally. Increasing attention is being paid to industrial and vocational education, which is also provided free, because of the important role this plays in equipping students with technical skills. Approximately 1 300 students attend the University of Mauritius at Le Réduit which, besides offering tuition in the arts and sciences, has recently expanded its facilities to include Schools of Law, Industrial Technology, Administration, and Agriculture. In addition, the Sir Seewoosagur Ramgoolam (SSR) Medical Centre has been founded recently and is providing medical tuition for students.

Many problems remain, however. Insufficient children attend preprimary schools. Too many children fail the basic Certificate of Primary Education examinations. There are too few students studying scientific and technical subjects. To overcome these and other deficiencies the education authorities have set themselves various objectives of which the following are probably the most significant:

• To provide a minimum of nine years' schooling for every child in Mauritius

• To streamline the education system and bring it more in line with the development needs of the country

• To promote the development of science, technology and business studies and to encourage greater research into the educational needs of a modern industrial economy

• To strengthen and stimulate the participation of the community in school life

• To raise the standards of any low-achieving schools and, at the same time, to make the educational system a fairer and more efficient one for all, and

• To increase cost-effectiveness by fully utilizing all existing school facilities.

Health and population development

Health and economic conditions of the population of Mauritius were generally poor during most of the first half of the present century. As a result of this, death rates were high and ranged between 30 to 40 per 1 000. In 1944, life expectancy at birth was estimated at only 32 years for males and 34 for females, while the infant mortality rate stood at a high 155 per 1 000. It was only after World War II that successful programmes against infectious diseases and malaria were implemented and this resulted in a rapid fall in the death rate to 15 per 1 000 in the early fifties. By 1952, life expectancy at birth had increased dramatically to 50 years for males and 52 for females.

Therefore, during the first half of this century population increase was minimal, indeed between 1901 and 1944 it only amounted to a total of 57 000, giving a low annual growth rate of only 0,33 per cent per annum. However, with the advent of improved health services after the war, the demographic picture changed rapidly. Fertility levels remained high, but mortality levels dropped and the population growth rate rose to 2,73 per cent per annum for the period 1944 to 1962. During this 18-year period the total population increased dramatically – by over 62 per cent (from 431 000 to 700 000).

This rapid escalation in population growth, which was obviously detrimental to development goals, led the country to adopt a policy of family planning which started producing satisfactory results by the end of the sixties.

The Mauritian Family Planning Programme is managed by two nongovernment organizations, the Mauritian Family Planning Association and Action Familiale in association with the Family Planning and Maternal and Child Health Programme of the Ministry of Health. Through their combined efforts and the changing socio-economic circumstances of Mauritius, the population growth rate fell dramatically to a rate of 0,79 per cent per annum for the last intercensal period, 1983 to 1990.

This reduction in growth rate was achieved primarily through a drop in fertility brought about by the adoption of family-planning principles (by 1991 contraceptive usage had increased to nearly 75 per cent) and the postponement of marriage. In recognition of the successes achieved in the field of population control and welfare, Mauritius received the Population Award from the United Nations Population Fund in 1990.

Mauritian population policy is to achieve Zero Population Growth (ZPG). To achieve this, the country's population policy sets out to balance sustainable socio-economic development with the enhancement of the quality of life of the country's citizens.

Family planning is thus seen by the Mauritian government as an essential component of a comprehensive socio-economic development strategy and, as a result, it enjoys full government recognition and support.

During the day the streets of Port Louis become rivers of humanity as people pour out of the buildings that line their pavements, in pursuit of their business.

ECONOMIC POINTERS

Diversification and export development

At the time of independence the Mauritian economy was dominated by a single crop – sugar. Over 50 per cent of the entire surface area of the island was under cultivation and of this over 90 per cent was under sugar cane. Sugar production in 1969, a year after independence, amounted to 675 000 tons. This one crop accounted for 93 per cent of the country's exports and thus it followed that any drop in crop production or lowering in the international price of sugar had a devastating effect on the Mauritian economy.

To add to the country's vulnerability was the fact that it had a very high level of unemployment and a rate of population growth that was unsustainable. Attempts were therefore made by government to stimulate economic growth and to diversify the economy. In 1970 a study group was sent to *inter alia* Hong Kong, Singapore and Taiwan to look at export-oriented countries. The group recommended to government that the country promote a programme of rapid industrialization by embarking on an entirely new approach to manufacturing, namely, the processing of imported raw materials into finished goods specifically for re-export. In December 1970 the Mauritian parliament passed the Export Processing Zones (EPZ) Act which provided the legal framework for this to be done. The Mauritian approach was simple – to provide a package of fiscal concessions and other incentives which would attract overseas manufacturing companies with already established markets to relocate their labour-intensive activities in Mauritius. Included in the numerous tempting incentives offered by the government to industrialists were tax-free holidays of up to 20 years, the option to repatriate all profits, and duty exemption on imported machinery, equipment and raw materials.

The Mauritian EPZ approach to industrialization was initially highly successful. Within one year, nine enterprises had started operations. By 1977 there were 89 factories operating in the EPZ, of which 52 per cent were textile plants. However, between 1977 and 1982 nearly one-third of the existing firms shut down. Part of the blame was due to oil price increases, a general downturn in world economic conditions, as well as strikes and political unrest in Mauritius. On the other hand, an excessive reliance on the textile sector, a rise in labour costs (which outpaced productivity) and other local factors also played a part.

In response to this situation the government launched a comprehensive structural adjustment programme aimed at deregulation and fostering economic development through further export-led industrialization, agricultural diversification and expansion of the lucrative tourist industry. In 1984, the Mauritius Export Development and Investment Authority (MEDIA) was established and specifically tasked to promote the export of products, services and investments, to develop and operate industrial sites and estates, and to plan, implement and review export-oriented manufacturing.

Mauritius is also a signatory to GATT (the General Agreement on Tariffs and Trade), the Commonwealth Agreement on Preferences, the General System of Preferences (GSP) and the Preferential Trade Area of the Eastern and Southern African States (PTA). It is a member of the ACP (African, Caribbean, Pacific) Group and as such is a signatory to the Lome IV Convention which permits tariff and import benefits into Europe for member countries. Through membership of these various trade and tariff agreements Mauritius is well equipped to offer its exporters substantial marketing advantages in a large number of key international markets.

As a result of the development measures introduced since independence, there has been a rapid and sustained expansion of the Mauritian economy. Real growth rates have reached as high as eight per cent. Total foreign trade increased from Rs10,7 billion in 1982 to Rs56,2 billion in 1991. Net foreign exchange earnings from the EPZ rose from less than Rs0,5 billion in 1981 to around Rs5,0 billion in 1990. Over the same period there has been a steady improvement in the country's balance of payments with the level of foreign exchange reserves of the Bank of Mauritius rising from Rs181 million to Rs13 billion. This expansion in the industrial sector has led to a rapid increase in jobs and to full employment. In fact, a shortage of labour has developed and wage costs are high relative to India, Bangladesh,

Despite economic diversification, sugar is still the cornerstone of the Mauritian economy. The industry is well catered for in terms of facilities and employs vast numbers of people.

A view looking across the beach at Club Méditerranée, which, like so many resort hotels, has its own special piece of paradise. Mauritius has a wide range of tourist accommodation and tourism has become one of the island's most important foreign exchange earners.

China and Vietnam. As a result Mauritius can no longer compete at the bottom end of the international market and is consequently entering the second phase of its industrialization process. This involves diversifying away from textiles and clothing (which currently comprise some 80 per cent of industrial output), modernizing its plant, equipment and technology, and competing at the top end of the market – where the island already has an edge.

Tourism

Tourism has flourished in Mauritius, becoming one of the island's most important foreign exchange earners, with income rising from less than Rs18,0 million in 1970 to Rs5,36 billion in 1993. The industry has grown from two beach hotels, one reasonable commercial hotel and various pensions in 1970, with only some 18 000 visitors a year, to 85 registered hotels (with another 19 hotels either in the planning or construction stage) and some 400 000 visitors to the island in 1994. In 1993 and during the first six months of 1994, the principal tourist-generating countries were France

(26 per cent) and Réunion (19 per cent), followed by Germany (11 per cent) and South Africa (10,8 per cent). Tourism from Europe is expanding rapidly as more and more Europeans 'discover' this subtropical island. In 1993, tourists from France led the way with 48 per cent of the European market, followed by Germany and the United Kingdom with the remainder coming from Italy, Switzerland, Belgium and Spain.

Mauritian tourism policy has shifted from the promotion of general tourism to specialist and elite tourism. Because of the physical limitation of space and the need to maximize income while minimizing environmental impact, government policy is to promote Mauritius as an upmarket tourist destination. Low-budget, charter flight-based tourism is not encouraged on the island, and no further hotel permits will be issued unless the proposed hotel offers some unique feature and caters essentially for the high-income, low-impact tourist market. Notwithstanding these restrictions, Mauritius is·anticipating an annual growth rate of 10 per cent until the year 2000, and the island's tourism planners

have good grounds on which to base this optimism: in 1988, the Mauritian government projected that the growth in tourist arrivals would reach 400 000 by the year 2000, but this figure will be reached in 1994. Unless there are major international circumstances that will adversely affect tourism generally, 600 000 tourists are expected to visit the island annually by the year 2000.

Tourism in Mauritius is based on a set of related assets. Firstly, its environment: spacious white beaches, the surrounding turquoise sea and the warm climate these assets bask in. Secondly, the relaxed and genuine friendliness of the Mauritian people. Perhaps the two most common expressions a visitor to the island will hear are, 'Don't worry' and 'No problem', and the beauty is that they are said with sincerity. Finally, the country's social and political stability, and the consequent lack of perceptible tension, make it difficult not to have a good and relaxed holiday on the island!

To maximize the country's physical assets all tourist hotels and related facilities have been built on or near to the island's wide beaches, its secluded coves and protected lagoons. Tourist hotels and bungalow accommodation are concentrated in three areas: in the west between Black River and Flic en Flac, in the north between Baie de l'Arsenal and Grand Gaube and in the east between Poste de Flacq and Grande Rivière Sud-Est. Two other holiday areas where the concentration of hotels and holiday facilities is less intense are the Le Morne peninsula in the southwest and Mahébourg/Plaisance in the southeast.

What Mauritius can offer its visitors is the opportunity to relax, savour moments of real freedom, and indulge in a wide range of water-related sports in places of romantic beauty, and to intersperse these activities with a visit to the bustling market in Port Louis or a hike in the mountains. At night the fun continues as there is a variety of things to do: enjoy a quiet drink while watching the sun's fiery death as it sinks below the surface of the sea, dine in one of the island's many restaurants, enjoy a romantic evening dancing under the stars, or tempt Lady Luck in one of the island's many casinos.

Infrastructure

The island has a modern infrastructure. It has a well-developed, if somewhat tortuous and overcrowded, road network which is being upgraded and expanded in order to cope with the increased demands in communication made by an expanding economy. Mauritius is served by an efficient and modern harbour in Port Louis, which has five deep-water, two fishing, and three litterage quays. It has a modern container terminal and bulk terminals for the loading of sugar, oil, wheat and cement. The government has embarked on a strategy to develop Mauritius as a regional trade centre in the Indian Ocean and to this end it is presently establishing a free port in Port Louis. Furthermore, substantial investments are being made in improving and developing the island's trans-shipment and bunkering facilities.

The country's only international airport, which is named after Sir Seewoosagur Ramgoolam and is situated at Plaisance in the south of the island, has recently been modernized. Air Mauritius,

the national airline, has at least one daily, direct, nonstop flight to Europe and several flights per week to India, the Far East and to various cities in southern Africa. The island is also served by a number of other international airlines, including British Airways, Air France, South African Airways, Singapore Airlines and Air Zimbabwe.

Mauritius is covered by a telephone network which is fully digitalized with computer-controlled electronic exchanges. An optical fibre cable network is presently being installed and international direct dialling facilities to most parts of the world via satellite are available to all subscribers.

Offshore facilities

With the rapid growth in the Mauritian economy over the last 10 years and the obvious need for its diversification, the government has committed itself to developing Mauritius as an international financial and business centre. Pursuant to this the country can offer: offshore banking, insurance and fund management; international financial services; a base for operational and regional headquarters; international consultancy services; shipping and ship management; and aircraft financing and leasing. To promote this business the Mauritian government offers a wide range of fiscal and other incentives.

Commitment to a free market

The Mauritian government believes in, and is fully committed to, the free enterprise economic system. It flirted once with socialism and found it untenable. Thus the role of the private sector as the creator and driver of the engines of growth is recognized and fully supported. Likewise, so too is the role of government acknowledged: to provide the basic infrastructural facilities and services required for growth and to sustain a sound investment climate.

With its successful economic diversification, industrial expansion programme and improvements in foreign trade, the island of Mauritius is upheld in many expert circles as a model for economic restructuring and transformation in a developing country.

PLATEAU TOWNS AND COASTAL REALMS

Port Louis and Pamplemousses

Port Louis is an amalgam of urban incongruence: modern, tall buildings with air-conditioned offices and elegant shops share a common road frontage with general dealers operating from single-storey wood and corrugated-iron shacks, built at a time that lies beyond the recollection of living memory. It has modern banks and advanced technology, but it also has old money-lenders who operate in obscure premises and on the shake of a hand. Men who go to work in grey suits and stiff collars rub shoulders on the pavements of the city with men who go to work in old sandals and open shirts.

A focal point for tourists is the market with its exotic oriental smells and fascinating merchandise. Here business has been conducted in the same premises and in the same way for over a century, only the pace and pressure has changed. Next to the market is Chinatown and the sense of the exotic continues. Mopeds and motorbikes noisily race past shops displaying names in bold Chinese letters, while inside, Chinese men and women wait patiently for customers to call. For a moment you could be excused for thinking you were in Hong Kong or Taipei. Within the heart of Chinatown is Jummah Mosque, the main mosque on the island. It was built in the 1850s when town planning was probably dependent upon the whim of some petty clerk.

Other notable places of worship within or near the city include the St James Cathedral, built in 1828 and which stands at the upper end of Poudrière Street, the Holy Sacrament Church in Ménagerie Street (built in 1879) and the St Louis Cathedral at the top of Sir William Newton Street. At Abercrombie just north of the city is Père Laval's shrine, while near the Champ de Mars is a Chinese pagoda. In Kwan Tee Street, to the west of the city, is the Kwan Tee Temple which is the oldest temple in Port Louis. Kwan Tee is a venerated warrior god who fought for justice. Traditionally, bank notes are deposited by the faithful and burnt at funerals and commemoration services as 'burial money'.

Port Louis bears unreserved witness to its colonial past. Standing boldly on its plinth at the entrance to the Place d'Armes (renamed Place Sookdeo Bissoondoyal) is a bronze statue of Mahé de Labourdonnais, his unseeing eyes fixed on the harbour across the road. Queen Victoria's statue stands at the other end of the Place before Government House, which once sought sanction for its laws from the peers of her realm.

The Natural History Museum and Mauritius Institute on Chaussée Street is an interesting place to visit. Perhaps its best known exhibit is a reconstructed dodo. In addition to this, there is a wide range of stuffed Mauritian birds on display, which gives the visitor some appreciation of the island's birdlife. The Institute's building used to be the offices of the Compagnie des Indes Orientales (the French East India Company). Next to the building was once the Jardin de la Compagnie, the company's vegetable patch, which today is a shady avenue of trees and statues, including that of the poet Léoville L'Homme.

On the outskirts of the city is the Champ de Mars, once a military parade ground and a place on which to promenade during the French colonial period. In 1812, shortly after the British became the island's new colonial masters, the Mauritius Turf Club was formed and the Champ de Mars became the island's first and only horse racetrack. The season is from May to the end of October; horse racing is a very popular sport and has become big business in Mauritius.

To the north, on a low hill bordering the city, is Fort Adelaide, which is also referred to as the Citadel because of its likeness to a Moorish fortress. It is one of four forts built by the British in the first half of the last century to defend the city against possible attack. The others, Fort William, Fort Victoria and Fort George, have either fallen into a state of disrepair or are inaccessible.

Perhaps the lasting picture visitors to Port Louis are left with is that of a bustling and purposeful little city that desperately needs a coat of paint and for something to be done about its crowded and narrow streets with their ankle-breaking pavements.

The central market in Port Louis was established in 1829 and is one of the city's most vibrant institutions with stalls selling merchandise and fresh fish, fruit and vegetables.

Sir Seewoosagur Ramgoolam Botanic Gardens These are situated about eight kilometres north of the city and were formerly known as the Royal Botanic Gardens. Also known as Pamplemousses, the gardens are situated in a region of the same name Originally the private property of a certain P. Barmont (or Barmond), acquired in 1729, the estate was known as Mon Plaisir.

In 1735 Mahé de Labourdonnais purchased Mon Plaisir and created a vegetable garden next to his residence. The garden was also used as a nursery for the planting and acclimatization of exotic plants, imported from Europe and the Far East, which were believed to have botanic and economic interest to the island. In 1739 the French East India Company acquired the property from Labourdonnais and planted virtually the entire estate with mulberry trees in the hope of introducing silkworms in order to create a silk industry. This proved unsuccessful. In 1767 Pierre Poivre was appointed *Intendant* of the island and occupied Mon Plaisir in his official capacity; in 1770 he purchased the estate in his personal capacity and immediately set about creating the present gardens. In addition to its use as an area

for acclimatizing exotics, particularly nutmeg and clove plants, the energetic Pierre Poivre introduced other exotics acquired during botanic expeditions that he sent to different parts of the world to obtain specimens which had economic potential and a good chance of surviving Mauritian weather and soil conditions. He also brought indigenous species into the gardens, as well as many of the palms which are such a notable feature today.

During the last century the sugar industry used the gardens to develop new cane species which were more suited to Mauritian conditions. In 1866, after a severe outbreak of malaria, the botanic gardens were used as a nursery for the planting of eucalyptus trees which, when rooted, were introduced along the island's wetlands in order to dry them out and so eliminate the mosquitoes' breeding grounds. In 1913 the Department of Agriculture took over the responsibility for the gardens and this is still the situation today.

Much attention has been given to the layout, design and the variety of plants, trees and shrubs in the gardens, and the result is an attractive feature that is a credit to Mauritius.

The North Coast

The North Coast stretches from Baie du Tombeau, situated north of Port Louis, to Grand Gaube in the northeast corner of the island. The long white beaches, calm sea and the lack of wind along the northwest coastline make it a popular area for tourists and as a result the greatest range of accommodation and number of tourist facilities in Mauritius are to be found here. In the northeast sector there are fewer beaches and so development is a little less intense.

Baie du Tombeau This sheltered bay in its setting of moderately high cliffs was named Bay of Tombs apparently because of the high number of ships that have been wrecked on this stretch of coast. The Rivière du Tombeau flows into the sea here and is believed to be one of the causes of the pollution which troubles this area from time to time. There are a number of small hotels and guest-houses catering mainly for locals and regular visitors from Réunion.

Baie de l'Arsenal To the north of Baie du Tombeau the coastline doubles back to create the secluded but very beautiful Baie de l'Arsenal, also known as Baie aux Tortues. The bay has two names as there were once a considerable number

The great water lily Victoria amazonica *spreads its giant leaves across one of the formal ponds at the Botanic Gardens.*

of turtles (*tortues*) that used to beach there to lay their eggs. After their demise at the hands of early sailors who sought their meat and the oil from their livers, there was no longer any point to the name; it became Arsenal Bay, after the French arsenal that was built there and whose ruins, together with those of a flour mill and lime kiln, can still be seen in the grounds of the luxury Maritim Hotel that has since been built on the shores of the bay. Set in a 25-hectare tropical estate, the hotel has a 500-metre beach frontage onto the beautiful Baie aux Tortues. Guests are offered superb accommodation and a range of sport and water-sport activities, including windsurfing and scuba diving.

Trou aux Biches To the north of Baie de l'Arsenal the coastline opens to become a long sweep of white beaches at Trou aux Biches. Here the coral barrier reef holds back the sea's naked energy, so these beaches are gently caressed by the waters of a tamed lagoon. Along their entire length groves of *filaos* trees interspersed with occasional palm trees provide shade and a break from a wind that very occasionally blows. Consequently, like bees around a honey pot, hotels, guesthouses, bungalows, villas and restaurants have gathered there.

The Trou aux Biches Village Hotel, one of the links in the Beachcomber chain of hotels, was the first luxury complex to be established there and it is still a favourite amongst many visitors to the island. Club Mediterranée followed, bringing its internationally popular holiday product to Mauritian shores. Since then a number of other hotels and other forms of tourist accommodation, catering to various levels in the tourist market, have been established. There are some who speak of Trou aux Biches as the 'Sunset Strip' of Mauritius, which may be so, but only in relative terms.

Pointe aux Canonniers North of Trou aux Biches lies Pointe aux Canonniers, which was fortified by the French in 1752 in order to defend the island from naval attack either from Port Louis to the south or from Grand Baie to the immediate north, and was used as a

naval harbour by the French. However, when the British expeditionary force launched their attack on the French in December 1810, they landed at Cap Malheureux. This is out of sight of Pointe aux Canonniers and the British attacked the French troops manning their seaward facing cannons overland from the rear. The skirmish was short and sharp and the cannons, pointing impotently in the wrong direction, remained silent throughout the battle. Today many of those cannons are still there, pointing out to sea, but they are no longer impotent: their function now is not to defend the island, but rather to commemorate this important chapter in Mauritian history. They also set the scene for the luxury hotel, Le Canonnier, which has been constructed around the old cannon emplacements and the fort the French built nearly 250 years ago.

Grand Baie This is the holiday mecca for Mauritians and tourists alike. It used to be a tiny fishing village that slept during the week and briefly yawned over weekends and school holidays. When the tourism boom began, Grand Baie was soon 'discovered' and was rapidly transformed as huge, medium-size, and small hotels, bungalows and villas were constructed on every possible site. Le Mauricia is built along the northern shore and stands on a promontory overlooking the bay, which even on a dull day is a rich turquoise blue; on a bright, sunny day the intense colour of the bay is almost beyond belief. Back-to-back with Le Mauricia, on the other side of the promontory, is situated the Royal Palm Hotel. At the time of writing, it was the only one in the region appearing on the listing of the Leading Hotels of the World organization – a recommendation that speaks for itself. Within a stone's throw of the Royal Palm, the Merville Beach Hotel fronts onto the beach and has views across to the islands of Coin de Mire, Flat Island and Round Island.

Grand Baie has a busy little business district, with a variety of shops including a shopping centre that has an active supermarket as its anchor store. There is a variety of restaurants, offering a choice of French, Mauritian and Chinese cuisine.

Pēreybère To the east of Grand Baie is Pēreybère, which is largely a residential area and a place where many of the island's rich have their beach cottages. There is also a number of smaller hotels, villas and bungalows for hire, restaurants to eat at and various public beaches.

Beyond Pēreybère, Cap Malheureux is the most northerly point of the island and the place where General John Abercrombie landed his troops when the British attacked the island. East of Cap Malheureux is the small bay of Anse la Raie where the Paradise Cove Hotel has been built. The only Indian Ocean hotel that is a member of the Small Luxury Hotels of the World, it makes use of the traditional architectural style of Mauritius and is set in a beautiful five-hectare, landscaped garden. Grand Gaube, to the east, constitutes the nominal border of the North Coast. Le Grand Gaube Hotel has been built around a semicircular white, sandy bay and adds yet another luxury hotel to the choice of superior accommodation that Mauritius has to offer its many international visitors.

North Coast Islands Lying offshore to the north are four islands which are generally considered to be part of the North Coast, although only in terms of excursions from the main island. They are Coin de Mire (Gunner's Quoin), Ile Plate (Flat Island), Ile Ronde (Round Island) and Ile aux Serpents (Snake Island).

Coin de Mire lies only four kilometres off the coast and is wedge-shaped, like that of the blocks (known as 'gunner's quoins') that were used in earlier times to raise the elevation of cannon barrels. Due to the island's precipitous sides it offers few places to land.

Ile Plate, a little further out than Coin de Mire, offers easier landing and good snorkelling. A small army barracks is situated on the island which is used as a training ground for the Special Mobile Force. The island also has a lighthouse.

Ile Ronde and Ile aux Serpents lie some 24 kilometres from Mauritius. Both of these islands are important nature reserves and access to them is restricted because of this. Landing is also extremely difficult because of the sheer cliffs that

drop into the water on both islands. Ile aux Serpents, ironically, does not have any serpents but instead is a renowned bird sanctuary. Ile Ronde, which is only 151 hectares in extent, has a great number of endangered flora and fauna species, including the Round Island hurricane palm and the bottle palm, both of which are endemic to the island. Endemic fauna species include a variety of small reptiles, and at least three species of birds breed only on this particular island. Since 1984, Ile Ronde has been managed as a nature reserve by the Mauritian government and the Mauritian Wildlife Appeal Fund.

The East Coast

The East Coast stretches from south of Grand Gaube to Mahébourg. The trade winds dominate this stretch of coast, bringing cooling breezes during the hot summer months and often bracing, if not strong, winds during winter. It is a beautiful part of Mauritius: the foreground is made up of rolling lands of green sugar cane, while in the background are the mountains of the Grand Port range and the peaks of the Blanche, Bambous and Creole mountains. And in the distance is the ever present, brilliant blue sea. Because of the onshore winds, the East Coast is generally wetter than the West, and, as a result, the plant and tree life is more prolific, thus adding to the region's general beauty.

The Legend of Paul et Virginie Lying less than a kilometre offshore to the north is Ile d'Ambre. Here the ill-fated *Saint Géran* ran aground in 1744, giving rise to a romance that has become woven into the very fabric of Mauritian life and folklore. This tragic moment in the lives of 208 wretched people provided the setting for French writer Bernardin de Saint Pierre's romantic novel, *Paul et Virginie*, which has been reprinted more than 500 times, and is credited with being at the forefront of the romanticism that was being ushered in, in French literature at the time.

The *Saint Géran* was a ship belonging to the French East India Company. It left Lorient in Brittany, on 24 March 1744, bound for Mauritius and Réunion Island

Coin de Mire (Gunner's Quoin) lies to the north of Mauritius. The wedge-shaped island is formed from layers of crumbling volcanic sandstone and, from the air, resembles a turtle.

and carrying 54 000 piastres which were crucial to Mauritius's faltering economy. In addition to other items of general cargo, there were also boiling vats and sugar-milling equipment which the then governor, Mahé de Labourdonnais, had ordered for the first sugar mill to be built on the island. This was to take place on his own estate, La Villebague.

Some 146 days after leaving France, the *Saint Géran* sighted Mauritius. Most of the crew were sick and weak from lack of proper food, while 13 members had already died of scurvy. It was late afternoon and even in their weak condition and sickness-induced lethargy a sense of excitement at the prospect of getting out of their oscillating gaol rippled through the ship's company. The ship's captain, Richard de Lamarre, knowing the condition his crew was in, did not want to risk sailing to Port Louis in the dark and attempting to anchor in the steady southeast wind that was blowing. He was persuaded by his Second Mate to heave to on the windward side of the island and wait for dawn – despite the protestations of the First Seaman, Ambroise, who knew the Mauritian coastline quite well.

Night fell and the wind grew less, all seemed quiet. But the sea's swell, driven on by a strong current, steadily pushed the ship landward. At three o'clock in the morning Pierre Tassel, the ship's watch stationed in the bows, saw what he feared most – land directly in front of him. He cried out to a sleeping audience, but it was too late; the sluggish, stricken ship continued to drift and it was not long before there was a sickening thud. The desperate peals of the ship's bell calling for help were carried in the wind, but no one heard. The lifeboats were cut free but the sea hurled them against the coral reefs. It was not long before the doomed ship began to part amidships. There was nothing left but for the ship's chaplain to administer a general absolution and give his final blessing to all.

Some managed to get across the reef and into the relative calm of the lagoon beyond, but the lack of food and consequent loss of strength, an inability to swim and the trauma of their harrowing experience led to many failing. Lamarre,

the captain, was washed off the piece of timber to which he was desperately clutching and was never seen again.

Two young maidens on board, Anne Mallet and Marie Caillou, had develped romantic relationships with two young officers, de Peyramond and Longchamp de Montendre, and when the ship began to sink, these two men gallantly tried to help the maidens to shore. But the girls' long billowing dresses dragged them down in the water. The men implored the girls to undress, but even at this dreadful time of crisis modesty prevailed and they steadfastly refused to appear naked before the men to whom they were not yet married. The sea eventually won its deadly tug of war and all four drowned. A total of 199 people lost their lives that tragic night.

Some 24 years after the sinking of the *Saint Géran*, Bernardin de Saint Pierre was sent by the French East India Company to Mauritius as the chief engineer of island fortifications. He did not like his job and clearly had aspirations to be a writer. He was to wait another 20 years before he wrote his romantic novel, *Paul et Virginie*, in which the young, beautiful and virtuous heroine Virginie is sent to France by the governor of the island to finish her education and broaden her horizons. She is heartbroken at the prospect of leaving her lover Paul on Ile de France and they each pine for the other. Virginie does eventually return, but her ship is wrecked on the island's coral reefs. Paul, on hearing news of a ship in trouble and suspecting that his beloved may be on board, runs across the island to where the ship wallows in distress and swims through rough seas to rescue his precious Virginie. After much effort, he eventually reaches her but is unable to save her as she is pulled down by the weight of the clothes she refuses to shed before the man she has not yet married...

This simple story was written at a time when romanticism was not yet in vogue, when the dangerous clouds of revolution were beginning to gather on the French political horizon and the uncertainties of change made any form of escape attractive. The naive and honest idyll of *Paul et Virginie* provided that escape for many.

A statue of Bernardin de St Pierre, author of Paul et Virginie, *the legendary novel based on the sinking of the* St Géran.

In Mauritius, as the slow passage of time gradually obscured the real events of 17 August 1744, Paul and Virginie became legendary and, as is the case with most legends, fact and fiction have become blurred so that the one is difficult to distinguish from the other.

A memorial commemorating the sinking of the ship stands at Poudre d'Or, a typical Mauritian village situated a little south of Ile d'Ambre. The fated ship has also given its name to one of the island's flagship hotels. Le Saint Géran Hotel is set on a peninsula, and has one side facing the sea, the other an inland lagoon which wraps around the hotel, creating an ideal spot for all forms of watersport. The hotel, one of three owned by the Sun International group in Mauritius, is undoubtedly amongst the finest on the island. Maximum use has been made of vegetation and its incorporation in a tropical garden that yearns to be explored. This in turn gives way to a Gary Player-designed nine-hole golf course on which there are no less than 4 500 palm trees. The hotel complex is a fitting tribute to the ship whose name it has taken and to the evocative memories it constantly creates.

A feature of the East Coast is the pre-ponderance of large, upmarket luxury hotels. As the region is relatively remote and at the same time blessed with long gentle beaches and protected lagoons, it provides an ideal setting. Each hotel is totally self-contained and guests need never leave its property other than to go on sight-seeing visits around the rest of the island. The major hotel developments on the East Coast occur between St Géran at Pointe de Flacq in the north and Le Touessrok at Ile aux Cerfs in the south. A limited number of smaller hotels and bungalow accommodation exists along this coast.

The drive from Le Touessrok to Mahébourg is interesting, attractive and different. The road hugs the coastline and passes through one untidy but quaint village after the next. Temples and mosques stand alongside one another, while neat square patches of labour-intensive market gardens bring order and symmetry into an otherwise chaotic landscape. There are small fishing hamlets built so close to the sea that they almost seem to be toppling into it.

At Pointe du Diable (Devil's Point), the name given to a headland which early mariners said was inhabited by the devil because of the strange effect it had on compass bearings, there are ruins of an 18th-century fort built by the French with cannons dating back to 1750. The fort, its walls more than two metres thick and commanding a view of the coastline from Ile aux Cerfs in the north to Ile aux Fouquets (with its lighthouse) in the south, was built to defend the French naval port at Mahébourg. Some of the cannons are still there, lasting ornaments of a forgotten era.

At Anse Jonchée, just south of Pointe du Diable, a signpost points to Domaine du Chasseur, a private nature reserve situated high up in the Grand Port mountains, which has a restaurant and accommodation for six couples in double bungalows. It offers guests the opportunity to walk in the mountains, hunt deer during the season, or go deep-sea fishing from Anse Jonchée. Its position in the mountains affords one breathtaking views of Grand Port Bay. It is hard to imagine that men could meet

Coral crushing takes place at Pointe des Régates near Mahébourg. Crushed coral is an important source of lime for building purposes on the island.

in such a tranquil and beautiful place to hurl abuse and instruments of death at each other, as the English and French did in 1810. In the distance, across the blue waters of the bay, is the burgeoning town of Mahébourg.

The South Coast

Mahébourg Once a thriving harbour town, Mahébourg's importance diminished as Port Louis grew bigger and its harbour busier. Today it is a somewhat tired commercial centre serving the southeastern corner of the island and its harbour provides home for no more than the little fishing boats that move up and down the bay. An important place to visit is the Naval Museum, housed in an old chateau that used to belong to the de Robillard family and which was used as a nursing home for those injured in the Battle of Grand Port. Here both British and French wounded lay side by side, convalescing from the wounds they had inflicted upon each other. Among them were both commanders of the opposing forces, Admiral Sir Nesbit Willoughby and Rear Admiral Victor Duperre, who eventually became good friends! The museum has several exhibits from the naval battle and a relief map

showing the complicated layout of the reefs in the bay where the battle took place. There are paintings, swords and some of the weaponry that Robert Surcouf – the romanticized 18th-century pirate known as King of the Corsairs – used during his swashbuckling career. The bell of the *Saint Géran* is also on display at the museum, as are several other items of nautical and naval history.

Near Mahébourg the Sir Seewoosagur Ramgoolam International Airport has been built, which is the point of entry for almost every visitor to the island. About five kilometres from the airport, beautiful Blue Bay has a varied coral garden that provides snorkellers and divers with vista upon vista of fascinating shapes and forms. Often the corals have hovering about them clouds of small multi-coloured fish, adding to the bay's fascination. The upmarket Shandrani Hotel, one of the island's finest, has been built around a cove within the bay and has a spectacular setting.

The South Coast is Mauritius's wild coast. There are no coral barrier reefs holding back the sea's restless energy, so it is unleashed directly onto the rocks and cliffs of the land. As a result, the coastline is broken and rugged, with steep cliffs that have been cut back by the sea to leave extensive marine platforms. These have been further eroded to form tidal pools and gulleys, each with its own ecosystem. A good example of this occurs at Gris Gris.

Further north at Le Souffleur the sea has not yet completed its task of cutting the cliffs back; it still rushes up to them, throwing its might against the lava rocks and cliff faces, attacking weak spots and thus sculpting the cliffs into stacks, archways, natural bridges and blowholes. In time these will collapse and leave behind marine platforms which the energetic sea will continue to gradually erode in its inimitable way.

Between Plaisance and Souillac the road, which is narrow and in a poor state of repair, passes through seemingly endless sugar-cane fields and occasional, conspicuously poor villages. At Souillac the Savanne river flows into the sea through an attractive inlet. There is a delightful little fishing harbour and restaurant at this point, a pleasant place to spend an hour or so.

After Souillac the road tortuously hugs the coast, and with gentle mountains on the one side and the blue sea, beautiful bays and white beaches on the other, it is hard to find greater natural beauty.

The West Coast

The West Coast stretches from the Le Morne peninsula in the south to Port Louis in the north. It is generally drier on this side of the island, so the vegetation is possibly a little less lush than on the East and South Coasts. The Le Morne peninsula was one of the first places where tourism took root in Mauritius and Le Brabant Hotel was one of the first resort hotels to be established. Today, with its sister hotel Le Paradis, the two form part of a large resort complex which offers its guests not only the attractions of a beach that seems to stretch forever and a sheltered lagoon, but also a wide range of sporting activities, including tennis, diving, deep-sea angling, horse riding and golf. Next door is the Berjaya Hotel, a large upmarket hotel that has been developed by a Malaysian consortium and consequently has a distinct and exciting oriental character and feel about it.

Silently brooding as it looks down upon the developments that have taken place at its feet, is the mountain of Le Morne Brabant. More of a gigantic rock than a mountain, it is imposing, not because of its height or size, but rather because of its precipitous cliffs which are said to be unscalable. However, early

in the 19th century a band of slaves managed to make it to the top where they hid from their masters. Whilst in hiding, slavery was abolished and when, one day, they saw troops preparing to climb the cliffs (presumably to tell them of their emancipation) the slaves panicked. Preferring death to capture, they hurled themselves off one of the cliff tops. The mountain thus became a place of mourning, hence its name, Le Morne, the 'mournful one'.

Chamarel Coloured Earths A few kilometres north of Le Morne is the village of Grande Case Noyale; here there is a turn-off to the Chamarel coloured earths. Shortly after leaving the village, the road climbs up the Savanne mountains, winding its way around hairpin bends and sharp curves, affording one the opportunity to look down on the sugar-cane fields stretching out below; across the translucent waters of the wide sheltered bay lies Ile aux Bénitiers, and Le Morne and its peninsula beyond.

At the top of the pass is Le Chamarel restaurant, built on an escarpment edge and commanding one of the most spectacular views in Mauritius. Just after the restaurant, a left-hand fork in the road leads on to the village of Chamarel, and the site of the famous coloured earths lying a few kilometres from the village. En route is the Chamarel waterfall, which is 83 metres high. Although spectacular and definitely worth a visit, it is difficult to get a good view of the waterfall in its entirety unless you are prepared to climb virtually to the bottom of the gorge.

From Chamarel the road continues to climb higher along the Savanne mountains and from various view sites one can look down on the beautiful Black River Gorges (Gorges de la Rivière Noire) with their forest-clad slopes, as well as Piton de la Petite Rivière Noire, the highest peak in Mauritius (828 metres). This area is to form the core of the proposed Black River Gorges National Park. The road then passes through forested areas and plantations; there is a turn-off to Grand Bassin, a holy lake for the Hindus, after which the road continues on to Vacoas and the other plateau towns.

The Chamarel restaurant has a magnificent setting on the edge of the Savanne escarpment, with wonderful views over the Le Morne peninsula and Ile aux Bénitiers.

Black River (Grande Rivière Noire) To the north of Case Noyale, Black River (Grande Rivière Noire) is an area that is well known for deep-sea fishing. In the summer months, between September and March, good catches of marlin, sailfish, wahoo, yellowfin tuna and shark are common. Centre de Pêche de Rivière Noire, a deep-sea angling club and hotel complex situated at Black River, provides a complete service to big game fishermen who come from all over the world to fish in these waters. Also in the area are factories which process the fish once they have been caught. Smoked marlin is a delicacy which, as already mentioned, competes favourably with smoked salmon.

Tamarin North of Black River lies Tamarin, named after the tamarind trees that were introduced by the Dutch and which grow in great profusion in the area. The village overlooks a tranquil bay into which the Rempart and Tamarin rivers flow; as a result coral reef development is minimal in the area, and instead, the waves of the Indian Ocean come crashing in with varied ferocity. Tamarin is better known for the salt that is produced from the evaporation ponds

that are found there. Before these were established, Mauritius used to import its salt from the island of Madagascar.

Flic en Flac To the north of Tamarin is Flic en Flac, which is rapidly becoming the Grand Baie of the west as more and more hotels, restaurants, bungalows and villas are built. There is some debate as to how the curious name Flic en Flac came about. Some say it is because of the large marsh that used to run parallel to the beach: as people walked through it their boots made a 'flic–flac' suction sound with each step in the mud. The more likely explanation, however, comes from the Dutch description of the area which was 'Fried Landt Flaak' (Free Flat Land) which was spelt in older maps as 'Fri-lan-Flac'; with the passage of time this changed to Flic en Flac.

Flic en Flac and the adjacent local authority of Wolmar (it is difficult to know where one stops and the other starts) comprise a long ribbon development of about five kilometres that follows the line of the beach and occurs within 300–400 metres of the water's edge. Accommodation ranges from the upmarket La Pirogue and Sofitel hotels through middle-range accommodation

offered by smaller hotels to self-catering facilities in villas and bungalows. As a result of the generally favourable weather conditions, the placid protected lagoons, long white beaches and wide range of accommodation, Flic en Flac is an important tourist centre that will undoubtedly continue to grow as tourism expands in Mauritius.

The Plateau towns
The island's central plateau is split into two halves by the motorway between Port Louis in the northwest and Plaisance. In the southwest is the Plaines Wilhems district, and in the northeast the Moka district. The Plaines Wilhems area has become rapidly urbanized over the last century and is the main residential area of the island. Effectively it stretches in one long conurbation from Beau Bassin outside Port Louis to Curepipe in the southeast. The municipal areas included within this conurbation are Beau Bassin, Rose Hill, Quatre Bornes, Vacoas, Floréal and Curepipe.

The history of urban development in Mauritius can be roughly divided into two eras: from early colonization to 1867 and post-1867. In the early colonial period the interior of the island was a dangerous place to live in because of disenchanted and runaway slaves, as well as others who had fallen foul of the law. Most people lived around Port Louis, but in 1867 a major outbreak of malaria sent thousands of people fleeing to the healthier highlands. The majority of Franco-Mauritians moved to Curepipe where the temperature can be as much as 5°C lower than in Port Louis. Those who could not afford to venture so far or were rejected because of earlier racist attitudes settled closer to Port Louis at Rose Hill, Quatre Bornes and Vacoas. With the passing of time the boundaries between these areas blurred as racial attitudes ameliorated, and land and population pressure erased any significance the boundaries may have had.

Curepipe The origin of the somewhat curious name of this favoured plateau town has been the subject of some conjecture. Some say it refers to the place where soldiers used to rest and clean

A view of the Grande Rivière Noire (Black River) industrial area with the mountain range of the same name rising in the background.

RODRIGUES AND THE OUTER ISLANDS

Rodrigues

Rodrigues is a small volcanic island only 18 kilometres long and eight kilometres wide. It lies some 560 kilometres east of Mauritius on a slightly higher line of latitude, namely 19°S.

Being of volcanic origin, its physical features are similar to Mauritius and it is also surrounded by coral barrier reefs. Since both islands are on almost the same line of latitude, the climate and vegetation is much the same. With so many similarities (including a high human population density), Rodrigues certainly has the 'feel' of Mauritius, but it is a Mauritius that existed before it was swept into the eye of the 20th century through modern industrialization and rapid urbanization. In addition, Rodrigues is largely 'undiscovered' and thus has a delightful sense of naivety and quaint charm which those tourists more attuned to cellular telephones, television and high-tech living may find unappealing.

The population, which numbers some 37 000, evolved mainly from liberated slaves and so, unlike Mauritius, its composition is more African than Indian. The population grew rapidly after World War II when the high birth rate continued after a substantial decline in mortality rates was achieved through the introduction of improved health services. The people of the island are predominantly Roman Catholic.

Past and Present Rodrigues' history is relatively uneventful. The Arabs were the first known people to sight the island, which they called *Dina Moraze*, and later around 1528 the Portuguese navigator, Don Pedro Rodrigues, was the first European to land there. The island was renamed after him. The first people to settle on Rodrigues were a small group of Huguenot pilgrims, who sought refuge from religious persecution in France in 1691 and set up home there. However, loneliness and the lack of female company drove the group back to civilization after two years. The leader of the group, François Leguat, returned to France after

An aerial view of Flic en Flac beach with the Pearle Beach Hotel built along its edge. This hotel is just one of several forms of accommodation offered to tourists in the area; there are also a number of self-catering bungalows and villas to choose from.

out ('cure') their 'pipes' whilst marching from Quartier Militaire to Port Louis; others say it takes its name from a town of similar name in the southwest of France. Curepipe's shopping, services and infrastructure are the most advanced of all the plateau towns and it therefore tends to attract most shoppers and tourists. The Trou aux Cerfs crater provides another reason for people to visit Curepipe. Situated on the outskirts of the town, the crater is a long extinct volcano that has become very heavily wooded. The wonderful views that can be had of the island on a clear day from this central point provide, perhaps, the greatest attraction. The Tamarin Falls, from which the island generates its electricity, found southwest of Curepipe, are also well worth a visit; however a permit

is required from the Central Electricity Board which is situated near the Kentucky Fried Chicken outlet in Curepipe.

Quatre Bornes, Vacoas, Rose Hill and Beau Bassin have nothing in particular to commend them to tourists, but a visit to Mauritius would not be complete without spending at least one morning wandering down some of their busy streets to see how many of the island's people live, eat, work and play. The shops are quaint – many are run-down wood-and-iron shacks – the music often unbelievably loud, the hooting incessant, the pavements usually nonexistent and the constant brush with passing vehicles an exercise in nerve control. But the smiles are broad, the warmth of welcome enduring, the memory of it lasting, and it should not be missed.

spending a number of years as a captive in Dutch-owned Mauritius for being an alleged spy, where he published a journal which gave a vivid account of their experiences and the conditions on Rodrigues prior to its exploitation. He recorded that the island had a rich fauna and flora, noting in particular the abundant giant tortoises and the existence of a flightless bird called the solitaire, which, like the dodo and the tortoises of Mauritius, were hunted to extinction by subsequent visitors and colonists. Likewise, the thick forests of Rodrigues were soon plundered for timber.

In 1864, bones of the extinct solitaire were found in the coral caves at Caverne Patate, situated in the south of the island. Various scientific expeditions were conducted in these caves and more bones were found. These were pieced together and a skeleton of the dodo-like bird was reconstructed, which is now displayed in the Museum of Zoology at Cambridge in England.

In 1725 a small party of men was sent to colonize the island in the name of Louis XV of France. The colonization of the island, renamed Marianne after the King's fiancée Marie-Anne Victoire, was a half-hearted attempt and it remained a backwater while the colonial tide swept through the rest of the undeveloped world. Because of this neglect there was no effective authority that could hold back the attacks on its resources by the privateers, corsairs and unscrupulous agents who constantly raided the island.

In 1809 British troops were sent to Rodrigues to take possession of the island in order to provide a base from which they could launch their intended invasion of Ile de France the following year. When the British defeated General Decaen in December 1810 and took over Ile de France (renaming it Mauritius), Marianne (which the British renamed Rodrigues), was included in the negotiations and the two islands were integrated administratively. Thus when independence was claimed for Mauritius in 1968, Rodrigues was incorporated as Mauritius's 10th administrative region – although a strong desire for independence is still harboured by many of the Rodrigues people.

The capital is Port Mathurin, named after one of the early French settlers on the island, Mathurin Brehinier, who is best known for the personal war he waged against the island's governor. Port Mathurin is little more than a hamlet; its CBD is about 600 by 300 metres in extent with English-named streets laid out in an ordered grid fashion. An adjacent area, Camp du Roi, is, however, being developed as the island's new administrative, commercial and industrial centre. The harbour comprises a jetty set into the lagoon, which is protected from the open sea by the barrier reef encircling the island, except where there are occasional breaks through which small ships and boats can pass. Shops in Port Mathurin are little more than general dealers; therefore anything special must be ordered from Mauritius, but with daily flights the delay is seldom more than a few days.

The capital has a wonderful *olde worlde* charm that those dictated to by their watches may find a little difficult to get used to. It also has a quality of life that should not be judged on the merits of affluence, but rather on the qualities of mutual caring and affinity.

Economy The economy of the island is based on fishing, subsistence agriculture, handicrafts and an infant tourism industry. This is boosted to some extent by subsidized food imports from Mauritius. The government owns 90 per cent of the land which is leased to individual families on 10-year renewable leases. The island's infrastructure is steadily being upgraded: it has direct dialling to virtually anywhere in the world, its health services are being raised on a par with those of Mauritius (it has one hospital and two large clinics), and education on the island is being improved through the establishment of an Education Centre, the building of a new secondary school, the upgrading of teacher qualifications and the conversion of the Technical College at Le Chou into an extension of the Lycée Polytéchnique of Flacq. The island's road network, while extensive, is not for the faint-hearted. It is a rugged island with roads to match, thus making a four-wheel-drive vehicle the preferred form of transport, particularly during the rainy season (late January to early April). Rodrigues is served by a diminutive airport at Plaine Corail in the south of the island.

The island of Rodrigues still relies on Nature's bounty for much of its income, and fishing remains one of the main forms of economic activity.

Some islanders are able to find employment at the coral quarry on Rodrigues.

Fauna and Flora The island's fauna and flora have suffered badly from the depredations of the past, while land hunger caused by the island's burgeoning population is making it difficult to redress the violation of the island's resources. After the forests were hacked down, exotics were introduced to fill the vacuum left behind. The result is that of the 38 indigenous plant species still to be found on the island, only two are not considered to be endangered as the quicker growing exotics vie for more space. The government has tried to combat this by fencing off those few areas where endemic species have superiority. These are to be found at Grande Montagne, St Louis, Anse Quitor, Mourouk, Pigeon and Cascades. The areas are weeded regularly and rare indigenous species, propagated in government nurseries, are planted throughout. It is hoped that these pockets of indigenous bush may be able to support some of the island's rare endemic fauna, such as the Rodrigues Warbler, Rodrigues Fody and Rodrigues fruit bat.

Tourism Until now, Rodrigues has been mainly for the intrepid and those truly wanting to 'get away from it all'. But the government, faced with the need to meet people's increasing expectations, has embarked on a programme of selective tourism promotion. A luxury hotel, the Cotton Bay Hotel, has been established at Pointe Coton where there is an excellent beach. No doubt others will follow. Over the years the best known hotel on the island has been the Hotel Relais Pointe Venus, which is an old 11-bedroomed colonial mansion built in 1870 and situated on a hilltop between Port Mathurin and Anse aux Anglais (English Bay). In his book *Golden Bats and Pink Pigeons*, Gerald Durrell wrote of this hotel that: 'It resembled nothing so much as an exaggerated film set for a Somerset Maugham story...' In addition to these two establishments there is a number of *pensions de famille* which offer accommodation.

Rodrigues has a handful of excellent dive sites along its coral reefs and a diving centre was recently established on the island. There are many opportunities for wreck diving as the island has had its share of shipping tragedies.

Rodrigues also has many interesting hikes, particularly around Mt Limon and Mt Malartic (390 metres), the highest point on the island. The caves at Caverne Patate, besides preserving the only physical evidence of the extinct solitaire, are also interesting to visit as they have some impressive stalagmite and stalagtite formations which are in a reasonable state of preservation.

Rodrigues has four little satellite islands, each of which is worth a visit. These are Ile de Cocos, Ile aux Sables, Ile aux Crabes and Ile Hermitage. The first two are nature reserves and a permit is required to visit them; this can be obtained from the Administrative Office in Jenner Street, Port Mathurin. On both of these islands noddy, fairy tern and frigate birds, amongst others, can be seen in fair number.

The Outer Islands

Cargados Carajos (or St Brandon) St Brandon constitutes a 22-island atoll which lies some 370 kilometres northeast of Mauritius. Fishing is the area's major activity, which is conducted by the Mauritius Fishing Development Company Ltd. There is no permanent settlement on any of the islands, so the fishermen are contracted for certain periods; they stay in camps set up on Albatross Island in the north and Coco Island in the south. At Raphael, which is a central island in the group, a small harbour has been developed and an administrative centre established. The atoll can only be reached by boat, however, as there is no island big enough on which to build a landing strip.

The Cargados Carajos archipelago, which, in the 19th century was privately owned, is well-known for its abundant fish and bird life, as well as its beautiful and undamaged coral reefs.

Agalega This is a 70-square-kilometre island, situated some 1 100 kilometres north of Mauritius. The island has been described as 'the queen of the oil islands' because of the number of coconut trees that grow there, including a local variety called *coco Bon Die*, which is very rich in oil. A copra industry has been established on the island and some 300 people live there permanently (of which approximately 140 are children for whom a new primary school is to be built shortly). Agalega has an old landing strip and plans are presently being considered for the establishment of a hotel on the island.

Chagos Archipelago For many years the Chagos Archipelago was administered from Mauritius. A few years prior to independence, no doubt because of the archipelago's strategic importance, it was annexed under the British Indian Ocean Territory and the main island, Diego Garcia, was leased to the USA as a military base for its Rapid Deployment Force. The islanders were removed, resettled in Mauritius and given financial compensation for their troubles; however there have been difficulties with their integration into Mauritian society.

Tromelin This is a tiny island lying about 500 kilometres northwest of Mauritius which is claimed by both Mauritius and France. No one lives on the island and it would appear that there is no urgency for either claimant to pursue her claim with any vigour.

PORT LOUIS & PAMPLEMOUSSES

Above: *Sculptured deities on the dome of a Dravidian temple.*
Opposite: *An aerial view of Port Louis harbour.*

Port Louis, which locals either pronounce as 'Paulwee' or 'Port Loo-is' is the capital and commercial centre of Mauritius and nestles in a basin with the Moka mountain range's jagged peaks providing a dramatic backdrop. At the foot of the city is Mauritius's only harbour, making Port Louis the commercial hub around which the rest of the island rotates. Almost all of the island's businesses have their headquarters in the city; the state legislature is located there and so is the bureaucracy. By day the city is hot, humid and boisterous; by night it is almost dead, as relatively few people are resident there. Most live in the plateau towns because it is cooler at the higher altitude, and they commute to the city daily. The result is large traffic jams in the morning and between 16h00 and 17h30 in the evening. The Mauritian capital is an interesting, small but thriving city that combines poverty with affluence, tradition with modernity, Eastern with Western influences, efficiency with disarming chaos.

Situated just north of Port Louis is the small village and administrative district of Pamplemousses, famous for its internationally renowned botanic gardens. Once known as the Royal Botanic Gardens of Pamplemousses, these cover an area of approximately 30 hectares and have been renamed the Sir Seewoosagur Ramgoolam Botanic Gardens in honour of the man who played a vital role in steering the country towards political independence and who became the island's first prime minister. Perhaps the most popular and probably the most photographed exhibit in the gardens are the giant Amazon water lilies (*Victoria amazonica*) which float gracefully on the surface of a large rectangular pond. The numerous and varied palms are another notable feature. There are 80 different species in the gardens of which some 25 come from the Mascarene Islands. Giant Aldabra tortoises, once a common inhabitant of Mauritius, are resident in the park as are deer which were brought to the island from Java over 300 years ago. The beauty, the interesting botanic diversity and the cool tranquillity of the gardens makes them a must on any holiday itinerary to Mauritius. Allow yourself at least two hours.

Above: A panoramic view of Port Louis looking across the city to the harbour in the background. The picture is taken from Fort Adelaide, which is also known as La Citadelle (the citadel) as a result of its likeness to a Moorish fortress.

Opposite left: An early evening view of Père Laval's shrine. The Lourdes of the Indian Ocean, his tomb is visited by Catholics from around the world. Laval, who was beatified in 1979, worked as a missionary amongst the poor and destitute on the island.

Opposite right: A ship leaving port with a view of some of the bulk loading facilities and extensions to the harbour presently under construction in the background. The modern loading facilities cater for sugar, oil, wheat and cement.

Above: Some of the tuna fishing fleet in Port Louis harbour. Mauritius provides a base for fishing fleets from the East, mainly Taiwan. In the background is a bulk grain storage silo.

Right: The statue of Bertrand François Mahé de Labourdonnais at Place Sookdeo Bissoondoyal (previously called Place d'Armes). He was appointed Governor in 1735 by the French East India Company and proved to be a man of great energy and foresight who did much to transform Port Louis from a primitive harbour to a thriving sea port.

Opposite: The General Post Office near the harbour in Port Louis is a national monument. It was completed in 1868 when Sir Henry Barkly was governor. Postal services began on the island in 1842 and these improved greatly when the railways were introduced in 1857. The architecture and character of the building reflect its British colonial heritage.

Top left: *Fruit being sorted out prior to sale in the Port Louis market. As Mauritius is a subtropical island, deciduous fruit does not grow here and so apples, peaches, plums, and others, have to be imported.*

Centre left: *Many thriving shops in Mauritius still reflect their humble origin. Businesses have passed on from father to son and they continue to fill an important niche in the market.*

Left: *Anthuriums do well in Mauritius and are grown commercially for export. Their beauty is to be seen in many homes, hotels and reception rooms throughout the island.*

Above: Many shops in downtown Port Louis are no more than pavement displays from which business is conducted with passersby. An interesting feature of many of these pavement shops is the large number of watering cans for sale. These are used throughout the island to irrigate small agricultural lots where the owners are not able to afford more elaborate piped irrigation schemes.

Right: Both Indian and Creole cuisine rely on chillies and strong spices for their distinctive and exotic flavour. Here dried chillies are on sale at the Port Louis market.

Above: *A visit to the herbal remedy stall is a must. Here a variety of herbs and* tisanes *can be bought which are 'guaranteed' to cure all manner of ailments such as diarrhoea, jaundice, piles, constipation, a lazy love life and so on. For those who are not ailing, there are herbs to make them even stronger!*

Left: *Sacks of vegetables being unloaded outside the Port Louis market. Fresh supplies are brought in daily, either from refrigerated sheds in the docks, in the case of imported fruit and vegetables, or directly from farmers operating throughout the island. Small-scale vegetable growing is big business in Mauritius and many homes supplement their income in this way.*

Left: *Fresh fruit can be purchased both individually and in bulk from many stalls in the Port Louis market. While many Mauritians buy their fruit and vegetables from the central market or from the smaller markets in Curepipe and Vacoas, many householders obtain their supplies from mobile greengrocers who bring fresh produce to the buyer's door. This service, which is seldom more expensive than buying from the market, is very convenient for those tourists who rent self-catering villas.*

Below: *Lottery tickets are sold at pavement kiosks. Mauritians love to try their luck and so lotteries are well supported and the sale of tickets is big business.*

49

Above: *Horses being led down the main straight to the starting stalls at the Champ de Mars racetrack.*
Top: *Throngs of punters gather around a betting kiosk to place their bets for the next race.*
Left: *The Champ de Mars racecourse, which is also known as the hippo-drome, nestles in a basin created by a sweep of the Moka mountain range, on the outskirts of Port Louis. Horse racing is a very popular sport and the Mauritius Turf Club dates back to 1812, making it the second oldest racing club in the world.*

Above: The road to the north from Port Louis passes a Chinese burial ground where elaborate memorials have been erected. These reflect an interesting mix of Christian and Chinese influences.

Right and opposite: All Chinese pagodas on Mauritius are situated around Port Louis. Ancestor worship is an important part of Confucian doctrine and the pagoda plays a central role in the rituals related to this religion. When a member of the community dies, the pagoda becomes the ritual meeting place where offerings are made and paper models representing objects valued by the person in life are burnt. It is believed that these objects 'pass through' the fire to join the deceased person in the other world.

Left: A colourful and decorative Dravidian temple in Port Louis. Approximately 53 per cent of Mauritius's population is Hindu, and of this, the majority comes from south India where the dominant temple architectural style is linear, or horizontal, and often incorporates more than one dome. Hinduism is based on three fundamental concepts: Maya (the vision of the world and its attractions), Karma (good works) and Samsara (reincarnation). Hinduism as we know it today is largely a fusion of the religions of the Aryan invaders from Central Asia who overran north India in the second millenium B.C. and the indigenous, peace-loving Dravidians.

Centre left: The finer detail of a Dravidian temple dedicated to one of the consorts of Shiva. The deities on the temple's domes are sculpted according to time-honoured rules that are contained in mantras. These inform the sculptor as to the general proportion, stature and appearance of each deity.

Bottom left: A simple Indian temple in Port Louis contrasts with the ornate splendour of the Dravidian one.

Opposite: A sculpted deity housed in a small roadside temple near Port Louis. Hindu deities are depicted in a variety of images drawing from both Dravidian and Aryan influences. Thus, animals, trees, mountains, rivers, male and female forces are represented, in addition to the inner forces of nature – sun, rain and fire.

Above: Inside the courtyard of the Jummah mosque in Port Louis. Islam is practised by some 17 per cent of the island's population, people whose forebears came from western India, including present-day Pakistan. The majority are Sunni and there is a small Shi'ite minority which includes a number of Ismailis. The Jummah mosque, built in the 1850s and situated in the middle of Chinatown, is the island's largest. It is intended to be a quiet place of meditation and prayer, rather than a tourist attraction, so tourists are generally not allowed to go beyond the courtyard. The main door of the mosque is carved from solid teak and is most impressive.

Right: The mosque's shoe rack. It is a requirement before entering a mosque, anywhere in the world, that each worshipper should remove his shoes as a sign of respect.

Left: The Church of St Francis of Assisi at Pamplemousses is built of basalt rock and its presbytery is said to be the oldest building on the island. The church itself is the oldest functional one in Mauritius, dating back to 1756. The parish cemetery contains the tombs of some notable historical figures, such as that of René Magon, the first French governor, Abbé Buonavita, Napoleon's confessor whilst he was an exile in St Helena, and Adrien d'Epinay who played a prominent role in local politics in the early nineteenth century.
Below: The simple but reverent interior of St Francis.

Above: *The Liénard Obelisk, which was placed in the Sir Seewoosagur Ramgoolam Botanic Gardens in 1860, is a graceful column of white marble donated by the adventurer and later natural scientist, François Liénard de la Mivoie. It was Liénard's wish that the names of the gardens' benefactors should be carved on it.*

Top: *Liénard also donated the splendid wrought-iron entrance gates to the Botanic Gardens.*

Right: *In addition to the great water lily of the Amazon, there are at least three species of Nymphaea, with white, pink and blue flowers, which can also be seen in the rectangular lily pond at Pamplemousses.*

59

Top left: *The huge floating leaves of the giant water lily, with their upturned edges, are a major attraction. The lilies only flower on two successive days each year. On the first day the flowers are creamy and have a delicious fragrance; on the second they turn pink and the fragrance is a little less strong.*

Left: *The peaceful, tree-lined avenues of the Botanic Gardens invite tourists to stay awhile and explore. It is not surprising that these gardens enjoy an international reputation.*

Above: Le Château de Mon Plaisir is not the original house that Mahé de Labourdonnais built. That building fell into disrepair and was knocked down. The present château was constructed by the English in the middle of the 19th century.

Right: Deer were introduced to Mauritius by the Dutch in 1639 to provide meat for passing sailors. Today only a limited number of wild deer are found in the south of the island; the rest are kept in small zoos, such as these at the Botanic Gardens.

NORTH COAST

Above: *Vibrant windsurfer sails.*
Opposite: *Some of the finest beaches in Mauritius occur along this coast.*

The North Coast stretches from Baie du Tombeau north of Port Louis to Grand Gaube. It is one of the island's principal playgrounds, with kilometres of white beaches caressed by the gentle waves of a translucent, turquoise sea. Baie du Tombeau, or 'Bay of Tombs', takes its name from the many ships that were wrecked there, and legend has it that pirates may have buried their treasure where the Rivière du Tombeau flows into the bay. Over the years treasure hunters have combed the region in the hope of finding buried loot from the past, but nothing has been found and the legend lingers on. North of Baie du Tombeau is the beautiful Baie de l'Arsenal, once known as Baie aux Tortues because of the multitude of turtles that used to beach there at night in order to lay their eggs. From Baie de l'Arsenal it is not far to Trou aux Biches which, not very long ago, was a quaint fishing village. Today it is the centre of a resort area attracting people from all over the world. A wide range of accommodation is available along the entire length of the Trou aux Biches coastline, from Pointe aux Piments in the south to Pointe aux Canonniers in the north. There is a number of excellent restaurants, a public casino and various places of interest, such as the Aquarium Centre, and a golf course.

Grand Baie, which lies to the north of Trou aux Biches, offers the most developed holiday infrastructure on the island. The bay itself is a coral-encrusted tropical lagoon with placid turquoise-blue waters that provide safe anchorage to a multitude of yachts, cabin cruisers and pleasure boats. Grand Baie is rightfully dubbed the 'Mauritian Côte d'Azur'. Lining the shores of the bay and its immediate environs are some of the island's finest hotels. In the small business district there is a supermarket, pharmacy, banks and a variety of shops. Some of the best restaurants in Mauritius are located here, offering French, Italian, Indian, Chinese, Japanese and Creole cuisine. To the east of Grand Baie lie Péreybère, Cap Malheureux (the most northern point of the island) and Grand Gaube. Here many Mauritians own beach cottages, and intermingling with these is a number of smaller beach hotels, holiday apartments, bungalows and pensions.

Above: Part of the day's catch. Mauritius has a wide variety of delicious fish and there are many seafood restaurants on the island. An interesting speciality that all visitors should try is smoked marlin, the Mauritian answer to smoked salmon.
Top: All of the major resort hotels offer their guests a variety of water sports, including deep-sea fishing, windsurfing, yachting, snorkelling, scuba diving and water-skiing.
Right: At the end of a day's fishing boats and nets have been prepared, and are lying ready for use at sunrise again the following day. After fishing until mid-morning, the fishermen will return to sell their catch.

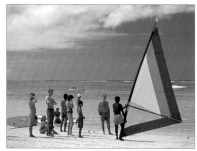

Above, top and left: *Mauritius's North Coast is holiday country indeed. Here, there are long white beaches flanked by some of the finest resort hotels on the island. Each hotel can offer its guests a variety of things to do, such as canoeing on the gentle aquamarine lagoon, windsurfing or yachting, diving, lazing on a pedalo, or simply relaxing in the warm sun on the silky beaches. For those who want to explore new horizons, there is a beautiful undersea world that can be experienced either by snorkelling in the lagoon's safe waters or scuba diving in the fascinating deep waters that lie beyond the reef.*

Top: *The* Isla Mauritia, *a 90-ton schooner that was built by Spanish ship builders in 1852, is one of the oldest sailing vessels in the world. Originally used to transport freight, it sank in 1959 under mysterious circumstances, but was refloated and has been restored as a sailing cruiser with modern, state-of-the-art equipment. It operates from Grand Baie and takes visitors on day cruises to different parts of the island.*

Above: *Passengers wait to be conveyed to the* Isla Mauritia *to begin a day of lazy cruising along the Mauritian coastline. The trip includes a barbeque on the pristine beach at Anse des Filaos, scuba diving along an unspoilt reef and musical entertainment by the Creole crew clad in period uniforms.*

Right: *The ferry nears the* Isla Mauritia *to fetch its passengers at the end of a lovely day of fun in the sun.*

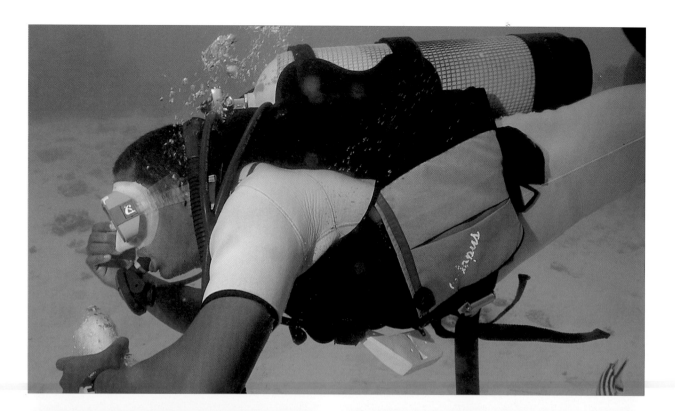

Opposite: *Scuba diving is well catered for in Mauritius. There are some 23 dive centres, each offering a variety of dive sites as well as training from a basic introductory course to senior certification. The centres, which are mostly based at resort hotels, are well equipped with modern gear and are professionally run by highly qualified divemasters.*

Top: *Divemasters accompany divers on every dive, ensuring that all safety measures are taken and that all dives are done strictly according to the rules of diving.*

Above left: *Soldierfish are very common in Mauritian waters. They gather in shoals and often seem to have nothing better to do than to watch divers with their big round eyes.*

Above: *Mauritius is virtually encircled by coral reefs which contain a variety of corals of many different species and types. Together these make up a world of immense fascination and interest. Some of the common corals to be found in Mauritian waters are staghorn, plate, mushroom, knob-horn, honeycomb, brain, turbinate and turret.*

Left: A colourful vegetable garden outside Triolet. Vegetable growing in Mauritius is labour intensive and not commercialized on a large scale. Small farmers thus take the opportunity to grow vegetables on the limited land available to them and allow entrepreneurs to market their produce at the Port Louis market or at roadside stalls. In this way it provides income-earning opportunities for a wide range of people.

Below left: Market gardening at Terre Rouge.

Below right: Irrigation furrows not only bring water to agricultural lands but are also a source of running water for the local people and a place where women can do their washing.

Opposite: Where irrigation is not possible, vegetable growers have to carry water to the fields and irrigate by hand. The production of these galvanized watering cans has become a thriving business on the island.

Above: One of the outstanding memories a visitor to the island will have is of little villages with a multitude of quaint shops. These often seem to crowd on to the narrow streets, which are always filled with people due to the lack of pavements. Here a family group wait for a bus to Port Louis.

Opposite top: Although Mauritius is part of the modern world, there is still time for friendship and discussion. Mauritian people are well known for their relaxed approach to life.
Opposite centre: A street seller in Triolet is surrounded by a colourful display of fresh produce.

Opposite bottom: One of the many delights Mauritius has to offer is an abundance of tropical fruits. While many of them are familiar to the international visitor, others conjure up images of exotic cocktails and days spent far away from the cold European winter.

Above: Nets hanging up to dry at the end of a day's fishing, at Grand Gaube in the northeast.

Left: Early morning, looking from Grand Gaube Hotel to Ile Ronde (Round Island). This island lies some 20 kilometres from the main island of Mauritius and a few kilometres beyond it lies Ile aux Serpents (Snake Island). Here one of those quirks of history must have happened, since Ile Ronde is not round and Ile aux Serpents has no snakes. The converse is true, however, which suggests that an early cartographer must have reversed their names.

Opposite: Sunset looking from the Royal Palm Hotel at Grand Baie.

Above: *Paragliding is a popular choice with tourists, and it is certainly hard to beat the thrill of soaring above crystal-clear waters.*

Top: *One of the lovely things to do in Mauritius is to hire a vehicle and slowly amble around the island, stopping wherever your fancy takes you, to relax under the shade of a tree or to sunbathe on the island's silky-soft beaches, and to swim in one of its endless turquoise lagoons.*

Left: *Hotel guests gather on the jetty at Le Canonnier Hotel, some to go diving, some to water-ski, some to go fishing and some to simply watch.*

Above: A panoramic view from Cap Malheureux which sweeps from the main island to Coin de Mire some six kilometres to the north. Some of the island's best scuba diving sites are located in these waters.

Left: The flame-red flowers of the flamboyant tree frame a lovely view across tranquil waters to Coin de Mire in the far distance.

Opposite: The Roman Catholic church at Cap Malheureux. It is at this spot that the British troops, under the command of General John Abercrombie, landed in 1810.

Left: Two Mauritian boys wash off the salt after a swim in the sea.

Below: A beautiful bay at Péreybère on the northern tip of the island. Péreybère, which is both a residential and resort area, is situated midway between Grand Baie and Cap Malheureux. There are a number of small hotels, guesthouses and villas to let in the area, and so it is a popular place for lower-budget visitors and guests on self-catering holidays. Over weekends and public holidays, Péreybère becomes very busy as people flock to the large public beach.

Left: *A number of fishermen operate from Péreybère and so, every day, it is possible to buy fresh fish directly from them when they come in with their catch. Fish are weighed on simple scales and the price is determined through adroit bargaining and the size of the catch that day.*

Top left: *Guests to Le Canonnier Hotel are welcomed by a blaze of colour and a driveway lined with soaring bottle palms leading up to the entrance.*

Left: *Basket and batik sellers seek out customers for their wares along palm-lined beaches. Only licensed sellers are allowed to sell on the beach and they have to conform to a strict code so that visitors and guests are not disturbed by unwanted and persistent salesmanship.*

Above: Holiday-making in Mauritius is an exercise in fun and there is certainly never a shortage of things to do. Here, a small group of guests at the Trou aux Biches Hotel are being taught how to windsurf.

Right: Much imagination has gone into the design of many of the beach hotels in Mauritius and a great effort is made to blend building and environmental design with landscaping and layout so that each complements the other in a unique way.

Right: *The cool verandah of the Royal Palm Hotel overlooking the sea at Grand Baie. One of the island's flagship hotels, it is a member of the Leading Hotels of the World organization and is one place where you are bound to rub shoulders with royalty, even during a stay of short duration.*

Opposite top: *A smiling waiter at the Royal Palm Hotel.*

Opposite bottom: *Pleasure boats at anchor in Grand Baie, the island's premier resort area. Some people have likened it to Mauritius's answer to Waikiki, although few would disagree that it still has some way to go! The centre of Grand Baie comprises a ribbon of shops, restaurants, hotels and a few night clubs, which follow the main road, Route Royale (Royal Road). The bay itself is not particularly well suited for swimming, except along the northern shores where major hotel developments have taken place. It is, however, renowned for its exciting yachting which is centred on the exclusive Grand Baie Yacht Club.*

Following pages: *A fisherman poles out to an anchored boat in order to bring it in for loading up with nets, prior to a day at sea.*

Above: In the early 19th century virtually every village in northern Mauritius had at least one magnificent plantation house, home to the wealthy sugar-estate owner. Their design and character was a rich blending of French and English colonial architecture and their opulence a tribute to the grandiosity of 18th and 19th century aristocratic Europe. Labourdonnais, which is one of the island's finest houses, was completed in 1858 and is situated at Mapou, near the end of the motorway from Port Louis.

Opposite: The driveway leading up to the Labourdonnais mansion is lined with Chinese banyan trees which were planted around 1820, and which undoubtedly led to a previous house that was built on the same site.

Right: Most of the grand plantation houses were encircled by cool verandahs which were bordered by striking balustrades decorated with intricate cast-iron mouldings. Since they are cool and capture the ambience of outdoor living, verandahs provide a comfortable place where the family can meet to relax and entertain guests.

Left: An aerial view of Château de la Villebague. This estate was purchased by Mahé de Labourdonnais around 1740 and the first sugar mill was established here some years later. The present house was built by Magon de la Villebague, a governor of Mauritius after Labourdonnais, and it was completed in 1759. The building was modelled after the governor's palace at Pondicherry and the formal gardens were laid out according to the symmetrical design of the gardens in the palaces of Europe.

Below: A view of one of the elegant reception rooms in the gracious Château de la Villebague.

Bottom: The centrepiece of the formal gardens at Villebague is a bronze statue of a stag bull. Hunting was a favourite pastime of Mauritius's landed gentry and was possible on most sugar estates. However, as land pressures mounted, so the areas for hunting diminished and today, only a few places are left where the sport can take place. These are restricted to the south of the island.

EAST COAST

Above: *A local boat-trip guide.*
Opposite: *Relaxing on a Mauritian beach.*

The East Coast stretches from below Grand Gaube in the north to Grand Port Bay in the south. It was once densely covered in ebony forests, but these were cut down by the Dutch for their timber, and sugar cane was planted instead. Rainfall tends to be higher along this coast, making it imminently suitable for the cultivation of sugar and, as a result, the region's rolling hills are covered in endless green carpets of waving cane with the area being one of the richest sugar-producing regions in Mauritius. The largest sugar mill on the island (said to be amongst the biggest in the world) is Flacq Union of Estates Limited (FUEL) which is situated a few kilometres from Centre de Flacq, the largest town on the East Coast. In the south, towards Mahébourg, sugar-cane production gives way, in places, to intensive vegetable production, their rectangular and square fields creating neat and colourful mosaics in the flat valleys of the Bambous mountains.

The East Coast is blessed with many long, white, powder beaches, protected lagoons and a rich, deep blue sea beyond the barrier reef. But this coastline is subject to steady onshore winds which occasionally strengthen, making it unpleasant to be on the beach or to use the sea for fun. As a result, hotel development has tended to be restricted to those areas which are protected from the prevailing winds. But windiness is relative – for most days of the year the wind is barely more than a cooling breeze which brings pleasing relief from the sun's often relentless heat. Lining the beaches are groves of casuarina trees which provide welcome shade, while the wind's soft whisperings as it passes through their filigree branches has a restful and even soporific effect on those who relax at their feet. The beaches offer lovely walks and it is not difficult to find moments of solitude when one can pause and reflect on the beauty and intricacies of creation.

Some of the island's finest and best known hotels are situated along this coast. Here relaxation is a way of life. Linking the hotels and the quaint, often higgledy-piggledy villages that lie in-between, is the coastal road which winds its way along the sea's shore giving motorists constantly changing vistas of sea, mountains and beaches.

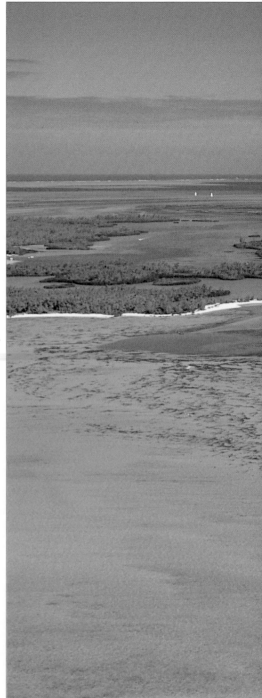

Top left: *An aerial view of Ile aux Cerfs opposite Le Touessrok Hotel. This island, reached by boat from the mainland, comprises some 700 acres of woodland where wild stags once freely roamed. It also offers excellent beaches and a shallow lagoon.*

Opposite centre: Le Touessrok Hotel is one of the island's most luxurious hotels. Its romantic setting on a small peninsula and adjoining island with fine, white beaches and swaying palms make it a particular favourite among honeymooners.

Opposite bottom: The hotel also caters for jetsetters and people who simply want to escape the stresses of modern-day life in comfortable and well-appointed surroundings. With nothing to do except enjoy yourself, the hotel is the perfect getaway.

Above: Sapphire waters gently wash against a rim of white beaches. In the distance the green coastal plain rises up to the Bambous mountains and in the foreground, Mauritian architecture makes Le Touessrok Hotel look like a fairytale castle.

Previous pages: *The St Géran Hotel and its magnificent nine-hole golf course have been built amongst 4 500 palms on a peninsula of silvery beaches embracing a blue lagoon.*
Above: *A bridge leads across to one of the islands built into the hotel's swimming pool, on which there is a poolside restaurant and coffee shop.*
Right: *An approach shot to one of the greens on the St Géran golf course.*
Opposite top: *The supreme luxury of idle days at a tropical resort: a waiter brings breakfast to late-risers on a lazy morning.*
Opposite bottom: *St Géran's beach is studded with grass umbrellas and the rustling fronds of palm trees.*

Above: *Guests relax in elegant cane chairs at the pool of the Belle Mare Plage Hotel.*

Left: *An aerial view with the Belle Mare Plage Hotel in the foreground. In the distance stretch sugar-cane fields dotted with piles of volcanic rocks and, on the horizon, the Moka mountain range provides Port Louis with its backdrop.*

Right: *Most resort hotels arrange for colourful displays of sega dancing. This exotic dance, accompanied by fast, rhythmic and exciting music, has deep roots in Creole history and is an integral part of Mauritian culture.*

Following pages: *A herd of deer running through a river at Domaine du Chasseur, a private nature reserve situated high up in the Grand Port mountains. It is the only estate in Mauritius offering controlled commercial hunting, used as an income and management measure.*

SOUTH & SOUTHWEST COASTS

Above: *Sugar-cane harvest.*
Opposite: *A bird's-eye view of the beautiful Chamarel falls.*

The South and Southwest Coasts extend from Mahébourg in the east to Le Morne in the west. Mahébourg was named after Mahé de Labourdonnais, the French East India Company's governor who placed an indelible imprint on the island over two hundred years ago. Mahébourg, pronounced 'May-bourg' by most, was once a busy port and naval base, but the constant southeast trade winds that blow in this area made it a difficult and often dangerous port to enter and navigate in, and so the island's harbour was relocated to present-day Port Louis. Although Mahébourg has a feeling of being past its prime, its role in the island's history can still be traced. Here, ships of the British and French navies met in anger and fought it out on the turquoise waters of Grand Port Bay: the ghosts of the past can still be heard by those who wish to listen.

Near Mahébourg is the Sir Seewoosagur Ramgoolam International Airport, Mauritius's only one, which provides the islanders with their major gateway to the outside world. Some five kilometres away is Blue Bay – a coral-filled bay with a name that needs no explanation. South from here, the nature of the coast changes fairly radically from that of the rest of Mauritius. Between Blue Bay and Souillac the long white beaches and placid lagoons give way to a sea that crashes, often wildly, against volcanic cliffs that line the shore. There are no resort hotels in this region, and indeed from Plaisance to Souillac the road runs well inland, thus depriving motorists of any views of the sea. It is possible, however, to go off the beaten track and to discover places of great geological interest, such as at Le Souffleur and Gris Gris, where the sea and the land have been locked in mortal combat over countless millenia, creating interesting and weird land forms in the process.

At the southwestern corner of the island a huge volcanic dome, Le Morne Brabant, stands guard over a pristine peninsula that extends out into the encircling lagoon. The Le Morne peninsula is the place where tourism began in earnest in Mauritius. It is here that one of the first resort hotels, Le Brabant, was built and the world was introduced to the beauty, tranquillity and relaxed atmosphere of this tropical island in the sun...

Above: *Transport boats, used to carry crushed coral to different building sites around Grand Port Bay, lie at rest at the end of a busy day.*

Right: *This memorial was erected at Pointe des Régates near Mahébourg in honour of the sailors who died in the battle between ships of the English and French navies off Ile de la Passe in Grand Port Bay, in August 1810. Ile de la Passe was heavily fortified, but the English managed to capture it through deception without having to fire a shot. However, they were subsequently defeated in the ensuing battle.*

Opposite: *An aerial view of Ile aux Fouquets with its lighthouse. It was on this island that François Leguat de la Fougère and his companions, the first settlers on Rodrigues, were imprisoned by the Dutch in 1693, having been accused of spying and smuggling ambergris.*

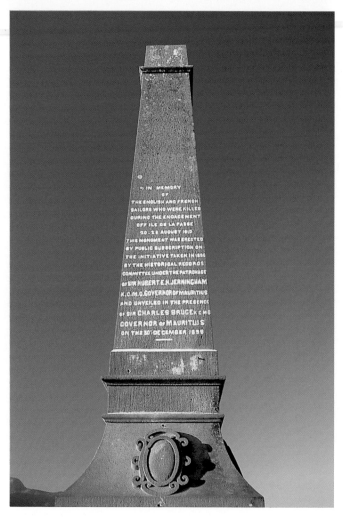

Left: *The South Coast has virtually no tourist infrastructure, thus few tourists visit it. It does, however, have places of great beauty and between Souillac and Baie du Cap, there are a number of lovely beaches interspersed with rocky outcrops, many of which have interesting tidal pools. The road hugs the coastline and it is possible to meander along, stopping from time to time to admire the view.*

Above: *Brightly attired sugar-cane harvesters wait for a lift home after a long day in the cane fields.*
Top: *This monument near St Martin's cemetery at Bel Ombre marks the spot where Charles Seabourne and 16 survivors landed in 1923. They had been adrift at sea for 25 days following the foundering of their ship, the* Trevessa, *some 1 600 kilometres off the coast of Mauritius.*

Above: *Sugar-cane harvesting in progress. As more people leave the sugar industry for employment in secondary and tertiary industry, so mechanization has intensified. However, there are certain places where the topography does not allow for machines and so harvesting is done by hand.*

Top: *Men transporting bundles of sugar cane home on their bicycles. These leafy stems will be used as thatching for their houses.*

Right: *These sugar-cane fields carved out of the hills above the beautiful Baie du Cap have been prepared for the new season's crop. Sugar used to be the only industry of any importance in Mauritius and the country's only real generator of foreign revenue. However, in the last decade or two, manufacturing and tourism have come to play increasingly important roles in the Mauritian economy. Nevertheless, sugar production is still of vital importance to the island.*

Above: *A beautiful Hindu bride.*
Left: *The hands and lower arms of Hindu brides are often intricately painted as part of their adornment for the marriage ceremony.*
Top left: Cavadee *is celebrated mainly by the Tamil-speaking Hindu community in honour of the Lord Subramanya. As part of the celebration, devotees carry a wooden frame decorated with flowers, which is known as a* cavadee.
Opposite: *About 300 000 Hindus make a pilgrimage every year to the sacred lake at Grand Bassin in the Savanne, where various rites are performed. This ceremony, known as Maha Shivaratree, is considered to be the biggest and most popular orthodox Hindu festival in Mauritius.*

Previous pages: *The coloured earths of Chamarel, which are also known as the Seven Earths, are one of the island's great tourist attractions. An interesting feature of these earths is that nothing grows on them and they never erode; the fiercest storm can lash the earths with its fury, but the rainwater simply runs off and the earths remain unaffected.*

Right: *A sweeping view across the southwestern coastline from the verandah of the Chamarel restaurant. This picture is only a small segment of the spectacular 180-degree panorama that awaits visitors here.*

Above: A panoramic view looking down the Baie du Cap river valley from the Savanne mountains to the deep blue Indian Ocean beyond.

Right: Cows gathering on the banks of the river mouth at Baie du Cap present a tranquil rural scene. However, pictures such as this are not as common an occurrence as one might think. Mauritius is a crowded island, thus farming has to be done intensively. As there is very little room for grazing, dairy herds are kept in feedlots, but whenever possible, they are taken out and given an opportunity to 'stretch their legs'.

Top: *The silent, ever-watchful Le Morne Brabant looms through a gap in the trees from the garden of the Brabant Hotel, which occupies prime land below the mountain and at the sea's edge. It is thus able to offer its guests not only water-related sports, but also land-based activities such as horse riding, golf and tennis.*

Above left: *Cruising around in small boats is always a favourite activity amongst hotel guests.*

Above right: *A close-up shows the intricate woodwork that decorates the gable ends of the luxurious Malaysian-owned Berjaya Le Morne Hotel, situated at the southern end of the Le Morne peninsula.*

Opposite: *Le Paradis Hotel appears dwarfed by the towering Le Morne Brabant. This mountain once provided a refuge for runaway slaves as its steep sides made their hideouts virtually impregnable. Sadly, when soldiers were sent to tell them of their emancipation, the slaves, fearing capture, leapt to their deaths.*

WEST COAST

Above: *The* dholok *is a percussion instrument used in sega music.*
Opposite: *The tranquil Grande Rivière Noire.*

A dominant feature of the West Coast is the backdrop of rugged mountains that line a steadily widening coastal plain, stretching from Le Morne in the south to Pointe aux Sables near Port Louis in the north. As with so much of Mauritius, the region also has its fair share of long, unspoilt beaches and tranquil lagoons and, with its reliable climate, it offers the perfect idyll sought by so many stressed city-dwellers. For those who want to lace their leisure with adrenalin-pumping action, the deep waters beyond the barrier reef in the southwest are rated by experts to be one of the finest game-fishing grounds in the world. Records keep tumbling as ever larger marlin, wahoo, tuna and reef sharks are hooked and hauled in by people who come from all over the world to enjoy the sport. Some of the best scuba diving in Mauritius is on offer at a number of dive sites that lie on the drop-off just beyond the barrier reef. For those who seek a different form of exercise there is hiking in the Bel Ombre-Macchabée forest and Rivière Noire gorges, while on the long white beaches and in the blue lagoons that line them the same range of water-related activities is available as at all the tourist resorts throughout Mauritius.

Flic en Flac, situated in the middle of the West Coast region, is a busy holiday village that is rapidly spreading along a five-kilometre stretch of tree-lined beach lapped by the gentle waves of a protected coral lagoon. The attraction of this beach has resulted in Flic en Flac becoming an important tourist destination and this, in turn, has led to the construction of a wide range of accommodation, from luxury resort hotels, to smaller high standard family hotels, guesthouses and private bungalows. In the village there is a number of shops which supply to the self-caterer and to tourists looking for souvenirs to take home. North of Flic en Flac lies Albion which is primarily a residential area. Here the nature of the coast changes quite dramatically as the white sandy beaches give way to rocks, while the barrier reef disappears and the sea loses much of its lustre due, among other things, to increasing levels of pollution. From Albion it is not far to Pointe aux Sables and the factories and hustle and bustle of busy Port Louis.

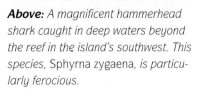

Above: A magnificent hammerhead shark caught in deep waters beyond the reef in the island's southwest. This species, Sphyrna zygaena, is particularly ferocious.

Top: Deep-sea fishing boats race out to sea at the beginning of the annual Marlin World Cup competition.

Above: Fishing is an integral part of Mauritian life. From an early age children learn how to fish and they miss few opportunities to throw in a line and try their luck. Here a group of children are fishing near Petite Case Noyale. On the horizon is the Le Morne peninsula.

Opposite: Mauritius offers some of the finest deep-sea angling in the world, with fish such as marlin, sailfish, wahoo, tuna and various species of shark migrating to its deep, warm waters between September and March. Here a Blue Marlin tops the scale at 255 kilograms.

FERTIGs ANGELREISEN
D-63791 KARLSTEIN

BOAT	ALBATROS III
ANGLER	Jörg J.
FISH	BLUE MARLIN
WEIGHT	561 LBS
LINE TEST	130 LBS
DATE	13.11.94
SKIPPER	CHRISTIAN

Above: At the Centre de Pêche, an angling club and resort complex dedicated to big-game fishing, boats and rods wait for fishermen eager to try their luck.

Left: A fishing boat makes for the fishing grounds in the deep waters off the Le Morne peninsula.

Top: A Blue Marlin offloaded from a ski-boat at the Centre de Pêche. The complex is situated on the shores of Grande Rivière Noire Bay and is thus ideally positioned for those interested in the sport of big-game fishing.

Top: An early morning picture of the salt extraction pans at Tamarin. Salt extraction is one of the oldest industries in Mauritius and is of considerable economic importance to the island. Sea water is pumped into huge open-air concentration ponds and the water is allowed to evaporate through solar action.

Above: Once sufficient water has evaporated, the salt residue is swept into piles, collected into baskets, bagged and sold as raw salt. It is a labour-intensive industry.

Right: An aerial view of the salt pans, with Montagne du Rempart, Trois Mamelles, St Pierre and Corps de Garde in the background.

Previous pages: A bird's-eye view of the spectacular stretch of beach at Flic en Flac, as small boats bob on the tranquil waters.
Left: An aerial perspective of the Sofitel Imperial with the jagged volcanic mountains of the central plateau providing a dramatic backdrop.

Above: Yachts with colourful sails are lined up for use by holiday-makers. In many of the resorts, most water-sports are available to all hotel guests at no extra cost.
Top: Cobalt-blue skies and an aquamarine sea – the ideal match for a perfect beach holiday.

Opposite top: *The pointed roofs of the Pearle Beach Hotel create an interesting pattern, etched against the limpid waters at Flic en Flac. The hotel is perched right at the sea's edge, and at high tide the gentle waves lap against the exterior walls.*

Opposite bottom: *Sega dancers make a dramatic and colourful entrance at the commencement of their performance. The sega has its origin in the rare moments of liberty when slaves entertained themselves at night on the beach.*

Above: *An aerial view of the casino and swimming pool of Sun International's La Pirogue Hotel. The imaginative architecture has been styled on the pirogue – the traditional fishing boat that was used for centuries by Mauritian fishermen.*

Above: Some 50 per cent of the island is covered in sugar-cane fields, and it is impossible to travel far without seeing green carpets of cane spreading out before you. The crop was introduced to the island by the Dutch in 1639 and since then it has played a dominant role in the Mauritian economy and way of life.

Top: The Pointe aux Caves lighthouse, situated on the West Coast, is an important navigational aid for ships approaching the island from the southwest and west.

Right: Sugar cane is either indigenous to Indonesia or New Guinea, the precise place of origin is not known. However, it has been used in India and China for at least 8 000 years and it is believed that the Chinese were the first to produce crystallized sugar from the juice of the cane. Since then, the cultivation of sugar has spread across the world. Here in Mauritius, the coastal plain provides a border of sugar cane for the majestic Moka mountain range with its jagged peaks.

Above: Domaine les Pailles, situated to the southwest of Port Louis, is a dynamic reconstruction of the past. Here, the old Mauritius has been recaptured and brought to life in replicas of the island's first sugar mill, an Alambic rum distillery dating back to 1758, a horse-drawn carriage typical of the last century, a spice garden, and three traditional restaurants. The casino, situated adjacent to the entrance to Domaine les Pailles, reflects interesting architectural elements from the past.

Centre left: A decorative detail from the wrought-iron entrance gates.

Bottom left: A railway line with a train and engine modelled on rolling stock used in the last century operates in the grounds of the complex.

Opposite: Girls in traditional dress welcome visitors to the estate.

Plateau Towns & Plantations

Above: *Eureka, a beautiful old Creole mansion.*
Opposite: *Volcanic rocks heaped amidst the sugar-cane fields.*

The plateau towns, as they are collectively known, include Rose Hill, Beau Bassin, Quatre Bornes, Vacoas, Phoenix and Curepipe. They are situated in the administrative district of Plaines Wilhems which covers an area rising gradually from the southern outskirts of Port Louis to an altitude of about 550 metres at the centre of the island. Until 1866, the island's centre was a dangerous place to visit, let alone live in, since it was mainly inhabited by runaway slaves and criminals fleeing from the long arm of the law. But between 1866 and 1868 a catalogue of disasters befell Port Louis, including cyclones, fires and disease (malaria) which drove wave after wave of residents away from the city to the island's higher and healthier plateau. As a result, the plateau was cleared of its recalcitrant inhabitants and steadily settled by an increasing stream of Port Louis residents.

Curepipe, situated at the highest point of the plateau and almost at the centre of the island, was the first town to be developed and today is considered to be the island's second most important commercial centre. It has 75 000 inhabitants and is an excellent place to shop for handmade model ships, duty-free jewellery, Indian silks and cottons, Chinese embroideries and handicraft, knitted woollen jerseys, and much more. Curepipe has the only European-style casino on the island and a splendid botanical garden that should not be missed. Vacoas, Phoenix and Floréal are suburbs of Curepipe, while Rose Hill, Beau Bassin and Quatre Bornes are separate towns or municipalities with democratically elected municipal councils. The island's industrial heartland is situated along a ribbon that stretches from Port Louis to Curepipe.

Some of the island's grand homes, which were part of the sugar plantations of Mauritius, are situated in or near to the plateau towns. One of these, Eureka, is a country house lying at the foot of Montagne Ory; it was built in the 1830s and purchased in 1856 by Eugene Leclézio, the first Mauritian Master of the Supreme Court. Today it is a museum that is open daily. Only four kilometres away is Le Réduit, which was once the Governor's residence but today is used by the military.

Above: *The causeway and bridge of La Nicolière dam, near Villebague. The water from this reservoir is used for irrigation purposes in the north of the island. Water is brought in by canal from the high rainfall areas east of Curepipe. The reservoir provides a favourite fishing spot for anglers.*

Right: *This rustic building served as the staff quarters and kitchen of the old Creole house, Eureka, built in the 1830s at the foot of Montagne Ory, near the village of Moka.*

Bottom right: *The notice outside the entrance gives a brief account of the house's history.*

Far right: *It is interesting to note the symmetry and the number of doors opening onto the verandah. In 1986 the house was turned into a museum and it is furnished in more or less the same way as it was in its heyday. There is also an art gallery on the second floor.*

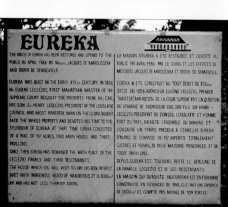

Above: The sculpted fountain known as La Fontaine des Arts is the work of two local artists, Neermab Hurry and Serge Constantin, and is situated in front of the Town Hall in Rose Hill. The complex houses a library, Le Plaza theatre and the Max Moutia Museum containing items related to Mauritian music and drama.

Right: An ornate gazebo is situated in the Town Hall grounds.

Opposite top: A balustraded stairway sweeps up to the side of the Town Hall.

Opposite bottom: The interior of the Max Moutia Museum has been likened to the foyer of an old English theatre. Some pleasant moments can be spent wandering around, looking at the posters of past productions and at sometimes faded photographs of the Mauritius Dramatic Club as it was in the thirties.

Above: *A solitary individual strolls through the sugar-cane fields near Vacoas with the mountains of Montagne du Rempart and Trois Mamelles rising in the far distance.*

Top: *The early evening light plays on the feathery flowers of the sugar cane while the central Moka mountain range provides a sombre backdrop. Sugar-cane flowers produce seeds,* but these are generally infertile, so propagation is carried out by using sections of mature cane. Rootstock is normally replaced every seven to ten years, depending on its condition at the time.

Right: *Low-angle sunlight creates interesting patches of light and dark on the sugar-cane-covered undulating plains of the central plateau.*

Above: The central plateau of Plaines Wilhems is the area where many of the craft centres on the island are located. A wide variety of baskets and handcrafted items are sold at different outlets throughout Mauritius.

Top: Intricately crafted model ships are painstakingly put together at a workshop near Curepipe. These miniature vessels are accurate right down to the last detail.

Right: At 550 metres above sea level, Curepipe is the highest plateau town in Mauritius and lies halfway between Mahébourg and Port Louis. Essentially a residential town, Curepipe is nevertheless attracting an increasing number of industries to its outskirts. Finding your way around can sometimes be frustrating, as streets are often unsignposted and houses unnumbered!

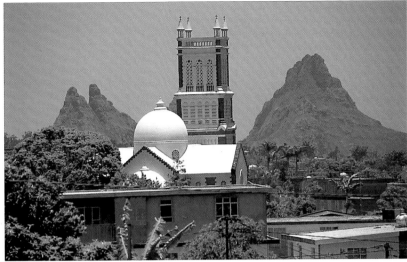

Left: The geometric layout of the sugar-cane fields east of Curepipe creates a fascinating mosaic of alternating shades of green and brown.

Top: The unusual shape of Ste Hélène Catholic church in Curepipe, one of the larger towns on the plateau, is framed by the rugged peaks of Montagne du Rempart and Trois Mamelles. The Basilica of Ste Hélène was built from funds donated by Hélène Naz, the daughter of a celebrated Mauritian barrister and plantation owner.

Above: The delightful all-wood Town Hall of Curepipe dates back to the end of the 19th century, when the town was given municipal status. In the foreground stands a bronze statue of Paul and Virginie, the hero and heroine of Bernardin de St Pierre's romantic novel Paul et Virginie. A popular residential area because of its cooler climate, the town also has most of the island's more elite shops and a population that is mainly Franco-Mauritian.

RODRIGUES & OFFSHORE ISLANDS

Above: The small airport at Plaine Corail on Rodrigues.
Opposite: Rodrigues fishermen laying their nets.

Lying some 560 kilometres east of Mauritius is the volcanic island of Rodrigues, only 18 kilometres long and eight kilometres wide. Its vegetation, topography, beaches and climate are much the same as Mauritius. The population of 37 000 people is more African than Indian in origin, and this relatively high number of people in relation to the island's size places quite a strain on Rodrigues' resources. The island's economy is based on fishing and subsistence farming, handicrafts and an embryonic tourism industry. Imports from Mauritius are subsidized and this helps to keep the cost of living down. The first known visitors to the island were the Arabs, who called the island *Dina Moraze*. They were followed first by the Portuguese, and then by the Dutch. French settlers arrived in 1691 and the British took over the island in 1809 as a prelude to their attack on Mauritius the following year.

The capital of Rodrigues, Port Mathurin, is little more than a village. Contact with the outside world is maintained through weekly shipping to and from Mauritius and daily flights from the island's diminutive airport at Plaine Corail in the south. The island's roads are rugged and undeveloped, and there is only one resort hotel. The tourism infrastructure is, however, being presently upgraded as more and more tour operators discover Rodrigues' charm and its ability to offer relaxed refuge to those seeking a moment's break from life's mainstream. A fascinating, almost forgotten island, it offers not only the delights of a tropical paradise in the sun, but also an opportunity to go back in time.

In addition to Rodrigues, there are four islands or island groups which are dependencies of Mauritius according to the constitution. These are the Cargados Carajos island group, comprising an archipelago of 22 atolls that lie some 370 kilometres northeast of Mauritius; Agalega, renowned for its indigenous palm, *coco Bon Die;* the Chagos archipelago and Tromelin. A military base has been established on Diego Garcia, the main island of the Chagos Group, by the United States of America; while Tromelin, although of little importance, is claimed by both Mauritius and France.

Above: There is one luxury resort hotel on Rodrigues, at Cotton Bay on the east side of the island. The hotel is at the forefront of Rodrigues' drive to develop its tourist potential.

Top left: The simple architecture of this Rodriguan home reflects the style typical of the island.

Top right: Rodrigues has a population of some 37 000 of which a high percentage comprises children under 14 years of age. Rodriguans have retained many of their own cultural traditions and much of their old folklore is still intact and actively passed down from generation to generation.

Opposite top: Although the people of Rodrigues are generally poor and their homes unpretentious, laughter and fun are commodities that are available in abundant supply.

Opposite bottom: The local stores are often quaint and filled with knick-knacks and handcrafted goods.

Previous pages: *Idyllic Ilot Gabriel. As a result of this island's isolated location, it was used in the 19th century as a quarantine station. Confusingly, one of Rodrigues' off-shore islands is also known as Ilot Gabriel and is famed for its translucent waters, gorgeous corals and prolific fish life. Other islands around Rodrigues include Ile Cocos, Ile aux Sables, Ile aux Crabes and Ile Hermitage. Ile Cocos and Ile aux Sables are small atolls and have been declared nature reserves.*

Above: *An aerial view of Flat Island (Ile Plate) and Ilot Gabriel which are separated by a shallow pass. Flat Island is situated off the north coast of Mauritius and has a coral reef which completely encircles Ilot Gabriel thus creating a lagoon. Both islands are now uninhabited, but a cemetery on the east coast of Flat Island testifies to the number of cholera victims that were buried there during the 19th century. Depending on weather conditions, it is possible to organize a trip to the island's lighthouse.*

INDEX

Page references in *italic* refer to photographs.